OVER 40
& YOU'RE HIRED!

This Large Print Book carries the
Seal of Approval of N.A.V.H.

OVER 40 & YOU'RE HIRED!

SECRETS TO LANDING A GREAT JOB

ROBIN RYAN

THORNDIKE PRESS

A part of Gale, Cengage Learning

GALE
CENGAGE Learning

Detroit • New York • San Francisco • New Haven, Conn • Waterville, Maine • London

GALE
CENGAGE Learning™

LIBRARY OF CONGRESS CATALOGING-IN-PUBLICATION DATA

Ryan, Robin, 1955–
    Over 40 & you're hired! : secrets to landing a great job / by
Robin Ryan.
        p. cm.
    ISBN-13: 978-1-4104-2554-6 (hardcover : alk. paper)
    ISBN-10: 1-4104-2554-1 (hardcover : alk. paper)
    1. Job hunting. 2. Middle-aged persons—Employment.
3. Career development. 4. Résumés (Employment) 5. Large
type books. I. Title. II. Title: Over forty and you're hired.
HF5382.7.R93 2010
650.14—dc22   2009051946

Published in 2010 by arrangement with Penguin Books, a member of
Penguin Group (USA) Inc.

Printed in the United States of America
1 2 3 4 5 6 7 14 13 12 11 10

FOR MOM & DAD
AND STEVE & JACK

PREFACE:
CAN THIS BOOK HELP YOU?

"Robin Ryan is the leading job search
expert in America today."
— NPR RADIO

Age discrimination does exist. So when you reach 40, you have a new career problem to worry about. Job hunting for most people is always a daunting task, and the older you get, the harder finding a new job can be. If you want to move on or up or even make a career change — and you've hit the BIG 4-0 or passed it — this book was written specifically to help you.

Face it, if you are over 40 and you want to land a great job, you have to approach the job search process — resumes, cover letters, interviews, and how you look for openings — differently from how you have before. You'll need a solid strategy and some additional support and insight to build your self-confidence.

Over the last twenty years, I've worked with more than three thousand over-40 candidates as career counseling clients. I myself have done a lot of hiring, and I'm constantly talking to the managers, senior executives, C-level execs, or board members who decide if you get hired or if they choose someone else.

My clients have tried these job search techniques and have successfully used the tools and strategies defined in this book to land new jobs. They learned the best ways to find opportunities; new ways to effectively approach a prospective employer; and how to successfully sell themselves. *The results speak for themselves. They got jobs — high-paying, interesting, terrific jobs!* That's the reason I believe this book will be a valuable resource to help *you* land the position *you* want.

I've worked with clients in good times, and in horrible economies. When jobs, industries, and fields they had devoted their life to disappeared. And still, they went on to find a new position, land a better career situation, and even secure a great salary. Why take a major drop in pay if you don't have to? They didn't, and if you want to preserve your lifestyle and prosper, you'll learn exactly how to do it in the chapters ahead.

Working together, I know we can make a better future happen for you.

— ROBIN RYAN

P.S. Special Bonus only for *Over 40 & You're Hired!* book buyers.

I created a special over-40 job search web-site section where pages are restricted to book buyers only. When you see this symbol, you'll find the URL address to the hidden website pages where you can access these special resources. You'll be able to download exclusive tools, forms, templates, charts, and salary surveys, plus the most up-to-date job listing websites I recommend for use in your search. You'll find additonal support to keep you motivated and inspired to reach your career goal as quickly as possible.

ACKNOWLEDGMENTS

You never know where great inspiration will come from. This time it was from Kristin Spang, my editor at Penguin. She must be credited with suggesting this book. It was her encouragement and ideas that helped spawn this work. We both share a love of our alma mater — Boston College — and it's been a joy working with her. I truly appreciated her championing *Over 40 & You're Hired!*

My clients are very important people in my life. They inspire me to try harder, and to continue learning new and innovative ways to help them find the success they crave. I am grateful that each has selected me to aid them in achieving their career goals.

I'm indebted to all the decision makers and HR managers who shared their insights so openly with me to enable my readers to be more effective and go out and land a great new job.

I have always wanted to help people and make a difference. But no one does it completely alone. A big thank-you goes to my staff. I could not have completed this project without the help of Dee Murphy, Sylva Coppock, and Wanda Bartel. Dee has been the creative source behind the Over 40 Web pages. She's a terrific assistant too, and I appreciate all her talents and efforts to help me help others.

A sincere thank-you goes to Heidi Harrington, who helped me out each day by bringing my son home from school so I could work uninterrupted. Her kindness was a big deal to me, and I appreciate her generosity. Two of my biggest supporters are John and Sunny Murphy — they help me in so many ways that just saying thank you will never be enough.

No matter what I do, it's my family that matters most. Jack and Steve — no one could love you two more than I do. It is your unconditional love, hugs, and support that enable me to share my knowledge in the hopes of helping many others find great happiness from whatever job they pursue. And for that I'll be eternally grateful.

CONTENTS

■ ■ ■ ■ ■

PART 1
IT'S A WHOLE
NEW BALL
GAME

■ ■ ■ ■ ■

"Success is a direct result of the
self-satisfaction that comes from
knowing you did your best to become
the best you possible."

ROBIN RYAN

CHAPTER 1
HIRING IS DIFFERENT NOW

"Put your best efforts forward
and you will succeed."

ROBIN RYAN

We'd like to offer you the job.

Those are wonderful words, words that every job candidate wants to hear. You can achieve this goal, but you will probably reach it in a much different way from how you looked for a job before. Times have changed, so you will have to change to get the outcome you want. It's a highly competitive world when you are over 40. Today's job market is most likely quite different from the last time you went after a new job. The process has changed. The younger competition is growing, and self-marketing is more important than ever before. Employers need talented workers, but when you are over 40, they have concerns — serious concerns — about whether you are up to

25

doing the job and giving them their money's worth.

When you are over 40, you must tap into the hidden job market (where 80% of all jobs can be found). You need to demonstrate your persuasive skills and have a terrifically written resume and cover letter. You must know the best ways to handle the tough interview questions — those they ask and the objections they may only be thinking about because of your age.

Hiring the right candidate can be a challenging task for an employer. Mistakes can be costly. Most people over 40 have larger leadership roles and so if they don't work out, the turnover often costs a company twice the person's salary, when considering loss of productivity, the expense of errors, severance, and recruitment costs to find a replacement.

To determine what actual decision makers think — the leaders, executives, and managers who decide your fate — I asked them. That survey, noted in this book, was very revealing. It was also different from what you may think. They identified the assets they see in people over 40; they noted key mistakes you'll need to avoid; and they mentioned their concerns and provided specific ways you can make a good impression. One thing became crystal clear: the bar has been raised. Your style, presentation, and approach must be contemporized to put forth the best *you* possible.

You have experience and accomplishments and have made strides in your career. But so have many others. On top of heavy competition, the job market becomes like a pyramid. The higher you go careerwise — i.e., director, VP, or CEO — the smaller the number of jobs available. And, as you have aged, you may have become more narrowly focused in your special field; many people settle into a niche, so they are an inch wide but a mile deep. But before you worry about being too specialized, getting too old, not having enough skills, growing overqualified, not wanting to relocate, or seeing your field disintegrating before your eyes, keep one fact in mind: you only need one job.

WHAT EMPLOYERS SAY ABOUT HIRING SOMEONE OVER 40

Age discrimination exists. It's illegal, but it does happen. Employers are savvy enough not to come right out and say, "You're old; we don't want you." But they may act on it by laying off older employees or hiring a younger worker because someone under 40 will work for a lower salary; may seem more eager, show more initiative, and have a fire-in-the-belly attitude; will likely have better computer skills; and may come across as more adaptable, less old-fashioned or stuck in their ways. But it does not have to be that way. Although we can't get in a time machine to take twenty years off the face and body, we can approach our job search in a different way. First we need to clearly understand what concerns a decision maker might have in his or her mind. Then we need to ensure that your style, process, and approach demonstrate that you are a terrifically talented person and they should jump fast and hire you.

I spoke to numerous HR managers, HR directors, and HR VPs. Their insights seemed much more generic but I have included their opinions because they too shape the hiring world and are often a company's gatekeeper or initial contact person.

My survey and conversations with actual decision makers were extensive and offer keen insight into the decision makers' thought processes. These CEOs, senior executives, directors, and hiring managers at various levels offered their opinions on hiring someone over 40. Many noted that a job seeker in his or her early 40s had an easier road than one in his or her 50s. But each executive agreed that they scrutinize the over-40 applicant much more carefully than younger prospects.

Let's get inside the minds of these decision makers. Even if you have hired many people yourself, once you are over the Big 4-0, getting yourself hired is very different from when you are the boss and you select someone else to work under you. Self-marketing is always more challenging because you must sell *you.* One top executive noted he personally hired hundreds of people over his career as a CFO but found a lot of age discrimination when he left his old position and began to job hunt at 57. "I still have some life left in me and contributions to make," he said. The problem was: did decision makers think so?

Here is a sample from the surveyed decision makers on the positive aspects of hiring people over 40.

THE PLUSES

Not everyone thinks mature workers are irrelevant. ("Mature" being the common HR term used instead of "older.") In fact, many don't. Numerous human resource managers I talked with pointed out several very positive characteristics of more mature workers, including:

- Having a superior work ethic
- Being loyal to their employers
- Exhibiting a more mature attitude
- Acting as strong role models and mentors to younger workers
- Offering superior customer service
- Being dependable — showing up every day ready to work (their kids are typically older or grown, thus they can work flexible hours)
- Being unlikely to need maternity leave

HR managers noted that bosses and organizations expect employees to be dedicated to, and focused on, their jobs. Commitment is essential! Sometimes employers worry that younger workers aren't as conscientious as older workers. Typically, baby boomers *are* hard workers and *are* more productive than younger workers. When you are a mature candidate, you must emphasize your commitment and high productivity level. Be sure to promote your assets by demonstrating to your prospective employer that you know how to get the job done and that you can be depended on to follow through with projects.

When it comes to job hunting over 40,

HR managers offer a more general perspective since they aren't the final decision maker (unless you seek a job in the HR department).

As I surveyed decision makers it gave me a new and much more comprehensive insight into who actually got hired and why or why not. Here are some of the positive aspects they named for hiring someone over 40.

- **GREATER DEGREE OF EXPERTISE.** Track records can be verified. Indeed it is experience that decision makers are looking for. They actively seek out those who are strong in their field because of their acquired industry or job knowledge. A CEO wrote that for her business, hiring people who are 40-plus is a big benefit. "They have the maturity to problem solve and work in the best interest of the organization more quickly and efficiently than many younger workers. They are more experienced in the field so they have greater 'market status' with our clients and customers. If they have a youthful attitude, that is a big plus — excitement for life, future, growth, energy and enthusiasm, that is a winning combination for professionals with us."

- **STRONG WORK ETHIC.** Baby boomers grew up in a different generation, with parents who pushed values like the importance of working hard. Employers really like that many boomers are highly productive and do go the extra mile on the job, where younger workers refuse to do much extra beyond the job description.

- **MORE BIZ CONTACTS.** Many executives feel that workers with a bigger Rolodex and larger circle of business contacts, developed over their career, is a *big* plus. Contacts are assets you have to offer that a less experienced (younger) applicant won't have had time to cultivate.

- **MATURITY AND PERSPECTIVE THAT ONLY COMES WITH EXPERIENCE.** Managing your way through bureaucracy and office politics takes years to navigate. The mature worker has more common sense and deals better with problems than 20-somethings do. You have a clearer understanding of the work culture and how to get things done. Younger workers often overreact to a challenge, decision makers noted. Mature workers often bring a sense that a challenge at work is not really the end of the world, but can be handled rationally. Mature workers seem to be better at solving tougher problems.

- **ESTABLISHED PATTERN OF RELIABILITY AND SUCCESS.** One CEO stated,

"I have hired hundreds of the over-40 sales reps. My decision is in a large part due to their age, and the value they bring with established contacts, and experience in the field. I found the more 'mature' sales rep was concerned about running a business and making money, rather than being caught up with being in the 'industry.' " Another wrote: "I have hired and employed many part-time staff in administration, particularly those that are already retired. My reasoning behind these hires is that they tend to be established economically and are looking more for activity than money, and they can be more reliable and a good influence on younger employees."

- **EXCELLENT PROBLEM SOLVING.** Older workers have seen and lived through more business cycles. They can see a broader, longer-range picture on a wider range of issues. They have also experienced good and poor economies. Many have seen different levels of staffing and tried different leadership approaches, and they seem to be better able to mentor those around them. Their maturity helps them to problem solve and work in the best interest of the organization more quickly and efficiently than many younger workers.

- **MORE LOYALTY TO ORGANIZATION.** The over-40 workers were cited for their strong commitment to their company and their willingness to do what needed to be done. They were less likely to be a clock watcher and do more for the company they worked for.

GETTING LAID OFF
WHEN YOU ARE OVER 40

Losing your job at any age is painful — oftentimes traumatizing. It is one of life's more difficult events, resulting in the loss of your identity, your friends in the workplace, your income, and your sense of security. No matter how well prepared you are, how supportive family and friends are, underneath any attempts at bravado there is a great deal of worry and self-doubt about the future. It's common to think, "I'll never get a job as good as I had," or "This is awful! — I'll never make that kind of money again."

Today is the age of downsizing and corporate cost-cutting. If you've found yourself out the door in favor of younger and lower-paid employees, you may be asking yourself, "Are my best days behind me?"

Not necessarily!

I taught outplacement classes to the Boeing Company's engineering/technical union. These were highly skilled professionals with deeply focused aerospace experience. And for each person, getting laid off was a difficult and challenging experience. They had very limited job search options, almost non-existent for some, since Boeing was the only place their type of job existed. Many attendees were over 40, with twenty-plus years at Boeing. The union followed up with an exit poll after my job search programs.

The classes I taught to the Boeing engineers and technical employees covered job search, interviewing, and salary negotiation skills. To the surprise of many, 80% of the laid-off engineers and technical workers moved on to a new job at a higher salary. Pretty good for employees who believed they'd have a lifelong career with the same company.

The results of the study for this group of laid-off workers revealed some significant facts:

- 80% obtained a higher salary at their new job. Only 9% ended up making less.
- Most salary increases amounted to 30–40% over previous salaries.
- It was reported that some doubled their salaries.
- Many of the workers left the aerospace industry completely.
- A large number noted that their new employers offered a more positive work environment that made them feel valued.

You too can overcome the perceived hurdles after a layoff. You will need to position yourself as someone who can get the job done and who brings a great deal to the table. Don't apologize for your age or joke about it or even mention it. Presume that your age is not an issue. Allow all your experience, skills, past accomplishments, and wisdom to shine.

RESILIENCE IS THE NEW
KEY TO YOUR SUCCESS

Industries disappear. Layoffs happen. Companies downsize or gobble each other up in mergers and acquisitions. Businesses fail. Jobs are lost. Bankruptcies wipe out jobs. Positions are terminated and outsourced. Financial problems force people to return to work after long gaps. The new business motto of doing *more* with *less* means more work with less people. The economy is revolting against excessive spending, and globalization makes everything much more competitive. Jobs are harder to find, especially a good-paying job when you are over 40. Millions of Americans suddenly find themselves on unemployment. Or hating a job and too fearful to even look for another.

If you are looking for the doomsday report turn on the news. If you are looking for answers to help you get out of this mess, and land a better or new job, this book is the solution.

According to Dictionary.com the word "resilience" means "the ability to recover readily from illness, depression, adversity, or the like."

That's your new frame of mind. You did

not make it past 40 without some hills to climb and valleys to walk through. Life is not easy. Tough as things may have been before, you survived and pushed on. Not easily — but you did it. Resilience is the trait that allowed you to bounce back. You are resilient, and you are about to move yourself into a better work situation.

Stop listening to the news — it's just too negative — and focus on making your life better.

PLAY TO WIN

Think of the job search as a game. It's a complicated game, but a game nonetheless. You are about to learn the rules, the short-cuts, and the hiring managers' insider tips that will help you come out a prosperous winner. You have unique talents and abilities to offer an employer, but to successfully market yourself you must understand the new job hunting rules. To land a better job, obtain a raise, or command a higher salary you must operate from the belief that you, as a worker, are talented and offer great value with your services. Employers pay more for *perceived value* just as consumers pay more for products they discern to be better. *Employers are willing to pay more for*

38

employees on whom they place a higher value. Therefore, *do not* underestimate your worth in the marketplace. Instead, stress it.

SUCCESS TIP: Your willingness to implement new strategies, focus, and hone your best skills in order to impress employers, using my proven techniques, is the key to your upcoming success in this career transition.

THINGS HAVE CHANGED, AND YOU MUST TOO

If you want a new job, you can find one. *You will need to change your approach, though, because you must move out of the pack to get noticed.*

You must be proactive in your efforts. In today's job market, these two things need to happen:

- You must tap into the "hidden job market" in order to find better job opportunities.
- You must use proven ways of better self-promotion that will get a prospective employer's attention.

Don't trip over obstacles you have placed in your own pathway. You must limit the restrictions you place on yourself during your job search. That means commuting, maybe working overtime, traveling — being open to going where the job is. The more obstacles you put on your next job, the more difficult it will be to uncover.

Know the exact job you want to be hired for. Be specific about what you want in a new position. Know the job title, if it's a lateral move, a step up, a big change, or even only a part-time position. Go after what you ultimately want, while remaining realistic about what is available in the marketplace. You must be flexible, and some of you may need to relocate to where you find the job. Keeping an open mind is the best course of action.

Networking is a must-use component for success. I will cover specific strategies for networking later in this book. Even if you think you *hate* networking, you will find this process an easy-to-use and valuable job search tool. It's also very different — gone are the days when you were sent to events and told to "work the room." Networking is now very strategic as you'll see in later chapters. Sadly, many people experience lengthy job searches because they are too passive in their approach. They look online and apply electronically. Click and send is easy, but not very effective. Whether you are extroverted and like meeting strangers or you're introverted, you can use the new networking process to help you land a better job.

Being proactive is imperative to succeed in today's job search. You'll learn to briefly present your top skills and strengths, and quickly tell a prospective employer about your past performance and results. In other words, you'll be ready to sell yourself at a moment's notice.

Your resume must be full of accomplishments and results. That is imperative because results are all that matters to employers. For those over 40, the big challenge is to include only relevant information, not your entire life's history. Writing a resume can be a major challenge. The Internet has made electronic applications easier, while at the same time it has created a black hole for resumes. Not only do you need a great one with appropriate key words, you need to know how to get out of the pack and in front of the eyeballs of the decision maker. And in a time when many people have stopped writing cover letters, you will need to create a very effective one addressing the employer's specific needs. Resumes only get a fifteen-second glance even when someone does see them, so yours needs to stand out and sell what you can do quickly and concisely.

The interview process has gotten harder when employers make snap decisions and have preconceived ideas about people over 40. The employer looks at your presentation — and sees your age first and worries if you are past your prime. The interviewer definitely notices how contemporary your clothes are and how worn-out you look or how engaged you seem. You'll need to counteract any age concerns employers have. Even if they don't ask — they are worrying about it.

Questions have gotten more difficult too. It's popular today to ask situational — often called behavioral — questions. You'll need to prepare answers in advance for these tricky ones, or you'll be stumped and likely get yourself eliminated in the process. Expect to get a screening interview, on the phone, long before you ever see a hiring manager in person.

Salary negotiations are more complicated since employers have many potential candidates to choose from. They have concerns that you are too pricey and may not produce the desired results for the dollars they pay you in salary. If you think that being older or unemployed prevents you from negotiat-

42

ing — you are wrong. In fact, employers are still paying good salaries to get the talent they want. You'll have to know exactly what your skill set is worth in the marketplace and what to say — and not say — to be effective in salary negotiations. By the time you are done with this book, you will.

Fact: Women still make 23% less money than men, according to the U.S. Department of Labor. This is a sad fact because women are reluctant to attempt negotiating. The initial salary offered by an employer can be increased if women apply the negotiation strategies and tools in chapter 18. Women *must* learn to negotiate, or they will continue to be underpaid in comparison to their male counterparts. The negotiation advice outlined in chapter 18 will benefit anyone — man or woman — seeking to get a better offer than what is initially put on the table. I have found that the first offer is usually not the best offer.

DOES IT WORK?

My clients land jobs. Of course they don't struggle alone, uncertain about what to do. They have me as their guide, just like you do now. My clients have gotten results. Many of them have gotten a much better job that paid significantly more than their last one. Now you and I are going to partner up and go through the process that I do with my clients.

This book is designed to help you excel in today's job market. Most likely, you fall into one of these five typical over-40 job hunting situations:

- You have been laid off or fear you will be.
- You dislike your current job and want another.
- You've been out of work, perhaps with a multiyear employment gap, and are now interested in returning to work.
- You are striving to move ahead and seek a promotion.
- You want to change careers, to find a more satisfying situation.

One thing you will learn in this book is that you need to exude an "I'm still a winner!" attitude. If you feel a bit disillusioned you may beg to differ with me on this point. Before you disagree, let me explain how I've seen older workers "wow" employers.

Over the years I've worked with many over-40 career-counseling clients and, frankly, some needed serious makeovers. Others transformed themselves, exhibiting an air of vitality and self-confidence that seemed to attract others, particularly employers. For example, Mary came to see me for interview and salary negotiations coaching. She was 69 years old. Her hair was completely white, and her face showed the lines and wrinkles of her age. Yet she was fascinating and vivacious, and she demonstrated exuberance for life. She had positive ideas that she planned to take to her new job. She radiated the confidence of a successful woman, one that any company would be lucky to hire. She scheduled four interviews and got four job offers!

Mary accepted one that put a very lucrative salary and benefits package on the table — a great salary *and* two extra weeks of vacation. Those four employers weren't *rejecting* her, they were *fighting* over her. Mary had mastered the secrets to self-marketing and used her strengths and talents to prove to the employer she was an ideal candidate. That is exactly what you will be learning to do in the pages ahead.

Fact: Compensation research reveals that the largest salary increases come when you accept a new job and go to work for a new employer. If you plan strategically, you can see a pay increase as a result of your career transition. I have seen hundreds of my over-40 clients do this. My clients are in *direct contradiction* to the Urban Institute study that reported workers 45 and older often land a new job, but with a 12–19% pay cut. My clients have been successful in improving their salaries and job satisfaction, using the strategies you will learn in the next several chapters.

Your success is just ahead — let's go for it!

Chapter 2
Now Aim

"Immense power is acquired by assuring yourself daily that you will succeed."

ROBIN RYAN

The smartest way to propel your job search is to know exactly what you are looking for. Take some time now to define your *ideal job.* You must have a clearly defined career objective. Think about what you truly want — in the short and the long term.

- What are your family and financial goals?
- What personal achievements do you want to accomplish?
- Who do you enjoy working with?
- What kind of responsibility do you want?
- What environment makes you most productive?

Give these questions serious thought. This

is a critical step in your decision-making process. Knowing the job title you plan to pursue, and the specific tasks you want to undertake, will make the search all that much easier.

LOOK BEFORE YOU LEAP

"Being paid well for something I would do for nothing — now that's lucky," says CNN talk-show host Larry King, referring to his own job. Luck usually comes from hard work, taking some risks, and making good decisions. Before you finalize your ideal goals, do some networking. Talk to other people in your field or in the positions you hope to acquire. Check out the future of the industry, new developments, trends, even new areas/fields/jobs you could leverage your skills into that are just emerging. This investigation is crucial to making sure the reality of living the job day to day matches your fantasy. Many people go to work each day with jobs that give them little joy. At this stage in your life, you need to find work that is rewarding and satisfying. Do this research *before* you get too far into your search, rather than finding out later that you hate the position you so actively pursued.

VALUES OFTEN DRIVE YOUR CAREER

Our values influence our decisions. Values are what is important to you, such as job security, salary, challenging work, being around interesting people, flextime, balancing work and family, etc. Our values can alter greatly over time. In your early 30s, you may be focused on moving up, obtaining more responsibility, earning a bigger paycheck, gaining recognition for your achievements. Wanting to be very successful may be a strong value you hold. Maybe your focus is in devoting yourself to helping other people. By 50, you may want to focus more on giving back to the community — starting service programs, doing work for non-profits, being a consultant, working with the sick or disadvantaged, etc. Others want to relax more and enjoy life by not working as hard as they did in the past.

What drives you today? What matters most as you shape your future? Take some time to determine what *really* matters most to you now. This affects the career choices you make and job positions you choose to pursue. It's a good guide when looking at job opportunities so your next position is a good fit for you.

CONSIDER YOUR INTERESTS

Incorporating your interests into the workplace often leads to greater job satisfaction. If you have a passion for music, then look at working in the music industry.

Are you interested in art? Perhaps you'd like to work in an art galley, or as a graphic designer. Are you a history buff? The country abounds with museums and historical preservation opportunities, if you know where to look.

Make a list of your specific interests; then prioritize them, marking five of your strongest interests. These are areas and fields to try to focus your job search on.

KNOW YOUR STRENGTHS

What strengths, skills, and special knowledge have you acquired in your previous jobs that will be valuable to your next employer? The best way to analyze this is to make a list of your strengths, skills, and special knowledge areas. For example, your list might contain some of these: coaching others, project management, negotiating sales, developing innovations, process improvements, researching data, selling, problem solving, organizing events, managing programs, product development, budgeting

— the list is endless.

For a more complete list of skills and strengths to choose from, you can go to my new Web page: WWW.ROBINRYAN .COM/BOOKREADER.

Since many people underestimate their own skills, ask close friends, coworkers, and family to contribute to your list, as they may recognize talents you have overlooked. Be specific. Note any special areas of knowledge that you possess. Maybe you are the expert on governmental regulations, or medical rehabilitation.

During your career, you have acquired valuable knowledge that makes you a more appealing job candidate. Identifying your talents and abilities enables you to clearly and succinctly explain what skills you would bring to an employer. You will also incorporate these strengths into cover letters, your resume, and interview conversations.

ANALYZE YOUR PREVIOUS JOBS

Examining your previous job duties will uncover your most sellable accomplishments. Write out what you did and list the things for which you were responsible. Note what results you achieved. Do this for all your previous positions. After you've finished making your list of job experiences, be sure you included:

- Important responsibilities
- Results you achieved
- Your greatest accomplishments

For example, did you save money by eliminating waste? Did you make money by cultivating new clients? Did you save time by introducing new efficiencies? Did you cut overhead by reassigning tasks? How did the company benefit from your accomplishments? As you begin to examine these, it will become easier to equate what you did with how it benefited the company. These are important as they will be examples you will share with a future employer.

Employers place great importance on experience when you're over 40. By working on these job descriptions, by going back and highlighting key points, you will clarify the talents you have to sell. Do these exercises for every previous job you've held and you'll uncover a gold mine of past experiences that will help you sell yourself to a potential employer.

VOLUNTEER EXPERIENCE MATTERS

More than half of all U.S. adults volunteer in some capacity. Review past volunteer efforts. Whether you were coaching a sports team, heading up a political action committee, doing presentations, or spearheading a fund-raising project, these credentials can add to your skill set. In fact, volunteerism might just help launch your next career.

Gaining marketable skills — paid or unpaid — matters to employers. Human resource managers repeatedly tell me that they value all kinds of experience and think highly of a person who has shown initiative through volunteer activities. Acquiring new skills — such as taking on leadership and management tasks — means better opportunities for you. Promotions often come about because you show the initiative to learn something new.

Professional associations offer superior options to volunteers, giving you the opportunity to network with others and to acquire new skills or perfect existing ones. Carefully select situations that will add value to your resume and make you more marketable. Whenever possible, volunteer to work on committees or projects where you can learn from a mentor. Being selective is the key to ensuring your skills will grow and lead to more career opportunities in the future.

When you're returning to work, volunteer experience can be a major bonus to add to your resume.

IDENTIFY THE "TITLE" OF THE JOB YOU ARE PURSUING

By age 40, you have acquired a significant amount of skill and experience. You could pursue any number of options. But the employer you are applying to will be hiring for a specific job. *Specific* is the key here. Don't make the mistake that causes so many people to derail their job search effectiveness. You *must* be able to define the *exact job title* you are looking for. No employer is going to look at your resume, with six pages of experience, and find you a place within their organization. You will have to identify the job titles that you would be interested in pursuing and that you are qualified to fill. For example, a senior executive applied to a hospital for both its open positions: for CEO and CFO. The recruiter quickly called to say, "Which search do you want to be included in?" When the candidate mumbled, "I'm qualified for both," the recruiter's response was: "Pick!" He went with the

CFO position as he had more qualifications for that role.

You must be articulate in identifying the job you seek, whether it's a systems trainer or a program manager in a large manufacturing company or a tax specialist with an accounting firm. Since the "hidden job market" seeks to get you directly in touch with decision makers, knowing the job title and level you are qualified to perform and the type of companies that need your expertise is step number one in the process for landing the best-fitting job.

Once you've identified the job title you want to pursue, you will begin your job search by creating a clear picture of your strengths, abilities, accomplishments, and values — learning new ways to sell yourself.

CHANGING CAREERS

If you want to look for a whole new and different career, recognize that taking on new challenges will require lots of time, a great deal of research, and likely additional training. In fact, many people over 40 are returning to college to seek new or advanced degrees. One client gave up a career in social work to become a graphic designer. She had always had artistic talent but never thought she could make a living until she learned how to create Web pages. She went back to college to get a graphic arts degree after she realized her creative skills, along with her new technical ability, would be a great bonus in her new career.

It is not uncommon for business owners to find new jobs in a wide variety of fields. One client closed his advertising firm at age 48 when his three biggest customers got gobbled up in mergers. He went on to become a marketing manager for a pharmaceutical company. You'll find people over 40 leaving their past jobs behind to go to law school. Others are in nursing programs, some pursue counseling degrees or MBAs, and a few even undertake extensive training and work on getting PhDs.

Not everyone goes back to college. Some take their skills and apply them to a new job title in a new field. They do this after a lot of networking and self-guided study to really understand the new field and see a potential place where they can contribute. For example, one teacher loved TV and video production. She retired at 52 and went into broadcasting to work on documentaries combining her interest in TV and love of exotic animals.

Certainly some careers can be aided by bringing along your transferable skills. By age 40, you have acquired many skills. For example, your project management skills can be used at any employer. Computer proficiency using software applications like MS Office are needed and beneficial in most jobs. Your strength in hiring good talent, leading a team, marketing a product — all these can transfer and are valuable to a new employer in a different field. MBA programs are full of people who are over 40. Military personnel retire and then go into new careers all the time. Educators leave the profession. There are so many options — the possibilities you can see are endless if you are willing to put in the energy to reach a new goal.

Women often leave behind their "mothering years" and pursue a new career after 40. Some try to pick up where they left off, but many look for a job in which they will find fulfillment in that it still allows them to blend work with their family. Many women seek to begin a new career once the kids have gone to college. For example, one client started her first career at 42 when her son went off to college. I worked with her on interview coaching and she landed an executive director position in a premier organization after several years of progressive and speedy advancement.

Career happiness comes as a result of aligning your skills, your values, and your interests. Do some self-analysis. What do you want to do? Where? Part-time or full-time? Read about job duties, growing career fields, and new industries on the Internet. Narrow down the career options that seem ideal for you. Make note of any skills you already have and new ones you need in order to pursue this change. It's better to identify your top strengths — these make working in any career easier because by using them you are tapping into your natural ability.

Be warned, this kind of a career choice is a significant endeavor. It is not what is referred to as a "job change," where the job tasks remain similar although the field changes, such as leaving an accounting job in manufacturing to move into accounting for a nonprofit.

A total career change is a major transformation. You are completely giving up one profession for a new one. It can be done, but you need to consider carefully the impact and personal costs of this career choice after 40. Explore this before you decide. Interview at least five people doing the job you'd like to do if you changed fields. This will help in knowing the "real job" versus what you think it may be. Many people seek out a career counselor to help them make this major decision. Consider that option if you need more direction.

"BRAND YOU" IS BUILT ON USING YOUR STRENGTHS

Personal branding refers to your career identity and professional reputation. It is not your job title. Brand You reflects other people's opinion of you. It can be a positive association, negative, or even neutral.

If branding can make or break a corporation or a product, just think what it can do for your career. Brand You must stand out, so employers eagerly seek to hire you. When the Gallup Poll conducted over eighty thousand interviews to examine why top managers excelled, only one common element emerged among all of them. Successful managers, the researchers determined, consistently used their strengths on the job. The conclusion here is that you should seek positions where you use your strengths to perform your job. You'll be much more successful and productive at work if you do.

By age 40 your natural talents have emerged in your work. You've applied and mastered your talents through repeated use. For example, demonstrated strengths might include great analytical skills; superior diagnostic talents; ability to write, to plan, or to build consensus; or creativity, team leadership, or public speaking.

Sell your mastered strengths. Most people under 35 haven't fully built their work competencies like you have. You do some things exceptionally well, and these are the key to establishing your personal brand and appealing to potential employers.

No matter what your profession, field, or industry, you can become the cream that rises to the top by advertising your strengths and becoming known for your unique talents and distinguished professional reputation. This is not faked or manufactured. It is the authentic and genuine you.

The first step in better defining Brand You really starts with your inner belief in yourself, and an attitude that you are special, have natural gifts, and offer great value to any employer. Self-confidence is a must. If you don't have it now, by the end of this book you will. To succeed when you are over 40, whether you want a complete change or you seek just to move on or up, the bottom line is *you want a rewarding job*. To achieve that goal, you *must* see yourself as special. Toxic negative thoughts and self-defeating talk will be a depressing detour that only drags out your job search. Spouses, relatives, even friends sometimes make you feel inadequate with all their questions, advice, or criticism. Don't listen to anyone who does not support and encourage you in your job search.

This personal branding process allows you to better define yourself. Work on writing out a concise, accurate description of who Brand You is, including your strengths and noted accomplishments at putting those talents to work.

To learn more about personal branding and career success, check out my personal branding website, WWW.SOARINGON.COM.

THE 60 SECOND SELL

Self-marketing is not a skill most people are born with. Of all the job hunting techniques I've ever taught, most job hunters state that the 60 Second Sell is "the best thing I ever learned." It's a key strategy in my book *60 Seconds & You're Hired!,* which teaches job interviewing techniques. The 60 Second Sell immediately captures and focuses the decision maker's attention on your top skills and abilities. This tool is used for networking and in job interviews.

The 60 Second Sell will help you target

your skills to meet the employer's needs. It allows you to summarize your most marketable strengths in a brief and concise manner. The 60 Second Sell is a *customized,* memorized statement that you target to meet the employer's needs. In 60 seconds or less, it summarizes and links together your top five selling points to perform that employer's specific job. Many clients have said:

- It was effective in capturing the employer's attention.
- It made networking much easier and more effective.
- It was very easy to use the formula.
- It provided a strategy plan for managing an interview.
- It was a great way to end an interview.

You need to be memorable when you network. A good 60 Second Sell will help you do that. For example, when you meet someone you wish to network with, you can clearly define who you are and what you do, to enable that person to aid you in your job search. Your 60 Second Sell, if you were a program manager like Dave, might sound like this:

I'm Dave Brodeau and I have ten years of experience in the wireless cell phone industry working as a program manager. In this role I lead cross-functional teams responsible for the development and delivery of new products and services.

In just a few sentences, Dave has told the listener who he is and what he does. He also broadened his options by not referring to his field as the "mobile industry," which many people outside his field might not understand; instead he says "wireless cell phone," which most people would understand.

If this were a job interview, Dave would elaborate and continue on with a more comprehensive and customized 60 Second Sell. In this situation, he's addressing the recruiter or decision maker and is making his pitch explaining how he is the best one to perform the job. The 60 Second Sell for Dave in his job interview might sound more in-depth, like this:

I'm a results-driven manager with ten years of experience in the mobile industry. I have a proven track record as a program manager responsible for the development and delivery of new products and services. I'm highly analytical and have both strategic and tactical experience managing product development and implementation teams. I excel at collaboration and can be depended upon to deliver new innovations, profitable products, and business solutions on time, under budget, and with outstanding quality.

You can be sure decision makers paid attention once he started his interview saying that. It caught their interest because he had clearly stated he had the skills needed to perform the job.

The 60 Second Sell is effective because it demonstrates your strengths and illustrates how you will fill the employer's needs. That is the key to its success, and yours. It is the most powerful way to start, and end, an interview. It's a convincing close and helps decision makers to define more clearly what you bring to the job — and remember it. This is a powerful tool you can add to your arsenal to help sell Brand You. Take the time to develop a good one. Read more about this tool in chapter 17, on interviewing.

CHAPTER 3
OVERCOMING
CONCERNS DECISION
MAKERS MAY HAVE

"The greatest barrier to success is
the fear of failure."

ROBIN RYAN

With any good marketing strategy, you have
to figure out how to overcome the objections a buyer might have to buying your
product. It's the same when you are selling
yourself. You need to spend some time
reviewing the following twelve potential
concerns that decision makers (DMs) may
have because of your age. Learning to
anticipate these objections, and get solutions, is the purpose of this chapter.

In my survey of DMs for this book, most
were very forthcoming with their concerns
about mature workers. And certain themes
were repeated over and over. In order to
better prepare you for creating a winning
resume, writing better cover letters, and
dazzling them in your interviews, I'm shar-

ing these concerns with you now. This allows you to realize what DMs are *really* thinking about a potential older worker, whether they voice it or not. By reviewing the concerns and the solutions, you can be prepared to counter and eliminate these potential deterrents to getting hired.

Some of these worries *may not apply* to you; some candidates *may think they don't apply* to them; and still others *realize* that they do need to prepare to answer these concerns. The fact is, this is what decision makers reported about older applicants in the survey. That is what makes it worthy of your attention. After each concern, I describe solutions that will help you negate their objections and turn these concerns into a nonissue.

COUNTERING THE CONCERNS

1. DM Concern: Declining Productivity Levels

Decision makers had witnessed a decrease in productivity with older workers. Some said a *significant* decrease. One organizational leader noted, "I see a lot of mature workers, and we hire many for my organization. During an interview, I watch closely for any candidate who seems lifeless, or who has a recent history of only putting in the minimal amount of work to get by. I want to hire people who know how to produce *now,* with recent on-the-job success. I must feel that they will perform fully in my position, or I won't hire them."

Whether they cared less, they no longer wanted to push as hard, life had drained their energy, or they had just gotten too caught up in outside interests, the bottom line was a noticeable diminishment in mature workers' levels of contribution. DMs said, "They just didn't have it in them anymore." One CEO said: "I want someone who can contribute *now,* not someone who did a lot ten years ago and still wants a large paycheck but has little to offer in adding to our results tomorrow."

Another comment repeatedly mentioned was that many over-40 workers were getting too much interference during work hours, and that lowered their productivity. Whether it was phones calls or having other (nonwork) stuff to do, DMs definitely saw some people had lost their focus on work and their performance was more marginal than exemplary. Too often their interests outside the workplace become highlighted in the interview and were perceived as demands. Time off seemed to move up on the importance list, a CEO noted. He went on to offer examples, saying family, children, activities, church, sports, vacations, etc., had taken a front seat over getting the job done well and showing initiative to deliver results and area improvements. Frequently, he wrote, candidates bring up these personal commitment issues during the first interview as requirements for considering employment.

SOLUTION: Almost every one of our top executives mentioned one key factor that will get you noticed and impress top management — *producing recent results.* It's *the* factor that influences decision makers. Show how you have recently applied yourself to a new and changing marketplace and been able to get the job done. In the chapters ahead, you will learn how to clearly state the results you have achieved in your resumes, cover letters, and interviews.

Examine your previous successes. *What results have I gotten in my past positions? What are my accomplishments?* Consider what difference your actions made. Did you save the company money or time? Start something new? Add to its revenues? These are the "results" DMs want to know about.

You will need to stress that you are *good*

at what they need done and that you deliver *results.* They want demonstrated initiative.

Decision makers stated they prize these traits: creative problem solving, integrity, honesty, hard work, achieving results, self-start ability, initiative, a positive outlook and attitude, and good communications skills.

They pointed out the need for employees who really think about improving the company, and who also can demonstrate, through past actions, that they have the follow-through to do the things necessary to benefit their company, division, or department.

Being recognized as a good, productive worker — dependable, with the initiative to improve and the ability to bring quality to your job — will make you more appealing to any organization.

It's never too late to be
even better than you are today.

2. DM Concern: Questionable "Fit" within the New Organization

Several decision makers commented that they wondered whether the older worker could blend into their office's culture. A high-level high-tech VP shared his perspective: "People engage differently when they are older. Those in their 20s and 30s in the tech world are comfortable using technology and doing everything by email. But often in older workers, they have a much different style and are much less likely to be email centered. Like most tech companies, email is the route we use to get things done here. This is a big work-style issue that some people can't seem to adjust to, especially if they are over 50."

Another DM brought up the issue of facing a young — sometimes a lot younger — boss. You might make that younger manager feel threatened. Some noted it might be just an internal fear but that the accomplishments, the level of "experience," and the larger network and contacts older workers had scared off younger supervisors. DMs worried about how the older person would respond under that younger person's leadership, and if a generational gap would be an issue. They were concerned that the person might be too stuck in their old ways. They questioned if the mature candidate could adapt quickly in dealing with coworkers who were younger. Several noted they were concerned it might present a rift in the current team if the over-40 person got the job.

SOLUTION: Research! Research! Research!

Know about the company and its culture. How do they operate? Can you adapt to that work style? Is it an environment where you can thrive? Look at the job objectively since every company's work culture is different. Learn what it's truly like to work at this organization. Type A personalities do not do well in slow-paced environments where it takes weeks to make a decision on tiny issues. Some organizations function at a much slower pace with less push and pressure; others change rapidly at a breakneck pace. Only you know what environment you thrive in, so use caution and investigate to find a spot where you do fit in.

Everybody has a boss, even CEOs. By this stage in your career you have learned the importance of getting along with the boss, whether you like the person or not. Your boss may be younger than your own child, but if you show your prospective new employer you are a professional, and give prepared examples of exactly how you communicate with your younger boss and other team members, this will effectively resolve this objection.

Most importantly, you'll be judged by *the results you have achieved.* In the chapters ahead, you'll get the necessary coaching so you'll be ready to offer any decision maker proof that you use your strengths to excel in any environment and that your abilities do achieve terrific results.

Every day do something that will
inch you closer to a better tomorrow.

3. DM Concern: Mismatched Skills for Job Needs

BusinessWeek ran a shocking article recently noting a surprising statistic: there were 3 million jobs that employers were actively recruiting for but so far had been unable to fill. Employers are finding a serious mismatch between workers' skills and employers' needs. People thrown out of shrinking or struggling industries such as construction, Wall Street, automotive, or retail — especially those over 40 — typically lack the skills and training for openings in growing fields like education, technology, accounting, health care, or government.

Don't expect this mismatch between employers' needs and the talent to meet them to get smaller. *BusinessWeek* noted the unemployment rate is likely to remain high because many people who want jobs will lack the appropriate qualifications. Economist Bruce Kasman stated, "A lot of relatively skilled full-time workers are losing jobs that are just not going to be there again. There is likely to be an unusually large skills mismatch." Employers need to bend as well, recognizing that the candidates they're seeking may not exist. One CEO wrote to say he's convinced the new road to hiring talent is to realize that "you as an employer are hiring based on 'potential,' and your company is going to have to let these people learn on the job, and train them."

SOLUTION: You must be a lifelong learner. You should be reading journals and the trend news for your industry. Even if you want to change into a new career or field, you can be self-taught on what is happening in that area, what skills are needed — and get those you are missing. Over and over again decision makers said older workers need continuous and new training to make them marketable. Many may not want to return to school, but if they want a new job they will have to. Do some research and look at the online job descriptions for the job titles you seek. What are the key qualifications? Missing something key? Maybe you can get a course online to teach you the needed skill. Maybe the position requires more management experience than you have. Think about volunteering to lead a committee to spice up your resume. If it's a computer application like Excel or Project then enroll immediately to update your skill set. If you really need a degree, maybe now is the time to look at classes (or better yet check into the affordable distance learning programs many state colleges and universities now offer).

Researchers at the University of Chicago found that as long as you stimulate your brain, it continues to grow and can process information ten times faster than when you were younger. An older person at 40, 50, or 60 will see patterns and find solutions more quickly, the study stated. It also noted that emotional well-being increases with age — so the older worker may experience less stress; feel less anxiety, anger, or worry; and be better able to go with the flow, demonstrating adaptability. Your life experiences and some of the tough things you've gone through have probably made you more resilient, flexible, and empathetic. And, according to the study, personal happiness increases with each new decade — all pluses to employers. As you grow older you are truly happier and wiser. That said, you must continue to read, stay up on industry and current events, and be sharp on the job.

One thing I've seen for sure is that *good talent is in high demand.* Employers are already being forced into bidding wars to recruit the few people who are qualified for the work (good news if you are the talent they want).

Do not let fear hold you back from
pursuing your dreams.

4. DM Concern: Lower Level of Expertise Using Current Technologies and the Inability to be Trained Quickly

Everyone who replied to the survey brought up this issue. Younger workers in their 20s and early 30s have much more natural aptitude on the computer. They grew up with it, understand it, and used it daily most of their lives. They love their techno-gadgets, which they claim make them more accessible and productive.

Some over-40 workers also have terrific computer skills. Some learn technology quickly, but many employers reported that the over-45 crowd displays a lot more technophobia. Maybe they haven't had to use it much before, but now their jobs are changing and they aren't catching on to new software programs or other technology devices as quickly as employers want.

"It's been unfortunate, but I've had to fire several over-50 female workers because they did not grasp using the new software fast enough. Although we gave them extra training and time, they couldn't get up to speed. Now, I'm extra careful and we test all future employees to determine actual computer skills," one health-care CEO reported.

I've worked with CEOs in their 50s who cannot send an email. They've had secretaries to do the computer work but, once unemployed, they are forced to learn or they may remain unemployed permanently. I've had new clients who could not attach a file to an email. They didn't know how to use the Internet or conduct research on it. Today decision makers want evidence of solid computer skills. They ask very specific questions in interviews and some even test computer skills before they make a hire.

SOLUTION: The world has changed and you must change too. You must learn to use technology — and fast! This is one area you have complete control over. First assess your computer skills. Determine what you need to improve on. Some programs are worth learning; others you won't need. Understanding how to research on the Internet is vital. Begin taking computer classes. Learn MS Office. Know how to use Outlook and attach files to email. If you are a beginner then race off and enroll in classes. Or find a tutor who can come to your house and teach you how to use the computer. You must get very comfortable using it — you can't let fear prevent you from acquiring these essentials skills. Don't let slower or nonexistent computer deficits cause you to lose out on a great job. Improve yourself — it will pay off.

Cell phones can do everything today. Maybe you don't want to be connected to everything — email, Internet, Yankee scores, etc. But if younger people holding your job (or the job you want) are doing these things, you need to learn how to do them as well. You don't need to learn how to set up this stuff yourself. Hire a kid to set it up for you, and once that's done, have him or her teach you exactly how to use it. If you are still stuck, go to the cell phone company store and ask them to show you how to use all the features. Take notes so you can later do it yourself.

Do not wish to be anything
but what you are.

5. DM Concern: Unwillingness to Move

More and more, over-40 workers, employers complained, do not want to move, regardless of the housing market. That lack of mobility hurts their chances for better jobs and promotional opportunities. Many decision makers said people are invested in their community or their family refuses to go no matter how great the new job is. Even when their type of job opportunities have dried up, these job searchers still refuse to broaden their geographical search, hoping to wait it out. Decision makers noted that is a bad strategy and people may find themselves unemployed a very long time. "It's really easy to find people that are 50% of what you are looking for," says a high-level IBM executive. "It's really difficult when you find a candidate that is 90% of what you are looking for and they refuse to move. This is a real dilemma." For many job seekers not relocating is a major issue. It often means they have to take a job locally that pays a lot less and will require a significant change in their lifestyle.

SOLUTION: In the past, when jobs went away people left the area and moved to where employers where hiring. That is no longer the trend. When the housing prices deflated, it left many people in a catch-22 about moving. They may have wanted to move, but their home wouldn't sell, or if it did, it was for less (in some cases much less) than they paid for it. If you are looking for a new job at a six-figure income, this is likely a situation you may find yourself in. You don't want to move, but where are the jobs for someone at your salary level and ability? Broadening your search to nearby cities or even nearby states can be a solution. You may be able to commute, or get a home in between where you are now and the new job one hundred miles away. Some people accept a job in the distant location and commute to the family's home only on weekends.

The bottom line is this: only you can decide what you will and won't do when it comes to uprooting and moving. The higher up your position, the fewer local options you have. You'll likely find most of your professional opportunities if you look in a wide geographical area.

So what are your options if you don't wish to move but can't find a comparable position locally? I've had clients who refuse to move — maybe their spouse had a job or their children were too involved in their school. Whatever the reason, they would not move to wherever the jobs were. In those circumstances here are a few of the options they employed:

1. **TAKE A DEMOTION.** One client's Fortune 500 company decided to move the headquarters to the Midwest from the West Coast. He was asked to move. His wife was seriously ill, so moving was not an option. He looked at the organization and found a job, two levels below his, that would allow him to stay in his current area. He decided that he would like the work and the job duties, so he proposed that he take on that job. His bosses agreed. He did suffer a salary cut, which isn't unusual. In other circumstances, people may alter their resume and tone down their accomplishments a bit, or remove an advance degree such as a PhD, to find something a step down. Others change industries, moving into a lesser role to remain in their current location.

2. **OPEN YOUR OWN BUSINESS.** This has a great deal of potential. The Internet allows so many businesses exponential growth opportunities,

and the Web doesn't care where you live. Franchises may be a terrific option. There are hundreds available and many are low-cost investments. Check out the website http:// entrepreneur.com/franchises. A fast way to be working for yourself is to buy an existing business. Check with brokers and research products and services you are interested in. Be careful to learn the demographics and market potential, and investigate if you think you can grow and make the business more prosperous. The next landscape design, spa, restaurant, storefront, or flower shop opening may be your own.

3. **DO CONSULTING.** This is a viable career path for anyone who has acquired a specialty or high knowledge level. Management consultants work in numerous fields and industries. Engineers, psychologists, educators, doctors, and PhDs can often be found working as consultants in their 50s. Joining an existing consulting group will make it much easier to get assignments, but you can start on your own. Look to former companies, old bosses, co-

workers, and even vendors you've worked with. Ask for introductions to land your first consulting assignment, and build from there. A terrific book on becoming a consultant is *Million Dollar Consulting: The Professional's Guide to Growing a Practice* by Alan Weiss.

You do have options! Spend some quality time considering: *what is the best answer for you and your career goals?* Keep this thought in mind: where there is a will, there is a way.

You only reach what you aim for, so aim high.

6. DM Concern: Disregard For Personal Presentation

A CEO from a major U.S. company noted, "There is a presumption that if your look is out-of-date, your information, skills, etc., are also out-of-date. Most over-40 job hunters have not had a makeover in ages and don't realize how off-putting their appearance can be, especially to a potentially younger interviewer or when they will be working with younger coworkers and/or customers."

On the other hand, a few HR VPs stated that sometimes people forget to act their age. They try too hard to look trendy, young, and hip, and it backfires. "A woman dressing like a teenager," one said, "comes off looking ridiculous. And men in an outfit their kids would wear does not work!"

Decision makers said, "Look professional! It's the best way to impress the decision maker across the desk from the interviewee."

Another sentiment was addressed by several decision makers and many top-level HR VPs. "We see too many people who are over 40 showing up at an interview and actually losing the job ten seconds into the interview. They have lost their enthusiasm for life, let alone the job, and when they walked through the door they look defeated and burned out." A CEO summed it up by saying, "My perspective is that they are looking for a final resting place with not much motivation to be an asset or help my company move forward. Don't think you can live out your dying days here."

SOLUTION: A dated appearance and a lack of enthusiasm were red flags for many decision makers. Many people over 40 could care less about fashion. It's not on the radar.

Their look, their selection of clothes, and their hairstyle often give off the wrong impression. Reinvention may simply mean for you to buy a more contemporary suit and update your professional appearance to throw off this stereotype. Undergoing a modernizing makeover is covered in detail in chapter 16.

Burnout is a different story. This needs some serious remedies. Time off, vacations, daily exercise, exploring hobbies you enjoy — maybe even counseling is necessary to get you out of this defeated mode. Depression can be a common issue. Are you depressed? Perhaps you need to see a physician to determine if there is anything physically wrong or to help you get out of the dumps.

Your attitude — positive, encouraging, negative, angry, or grumpy — has a big impact on those around you. DMs want people who don't cause problems with coworkers. A great many of these employers commented that a bad attitude was often the reason they skipped over hiring someone over 40. (Many did add that they didn't want anyone at any age with a lousy attitude.)

If you aren't upbeat, try these things to improve your mood. Surround yourself with uplifting music, funny TV shows, and movies with victorious characters and happy endings. If your poor outlook is more deeply rooted, see a counselor. Read books on having a positive attitude so your lack of smiles doesn't keep you from being hired.

Action is a great cure for fear.

7. DM Concern: Old-Fashioned Management Style

Decision makers warned about seeing definite "biases" that managers and executives, including C-level candidates, have. Many job seekers don't realize how they are perceived in a conversation, but these biases come through. DMs noticed it particularly when discussing managing styles and how people should or shouldn't work. The older supervisor often came across as much more judgmental and seemed likely to demand more face time. He or she seemed not flexible enough to allow the employees under him or her to work in their own style with autonomy to get the job done. Employees like collaboration and teamwork, and most do better with some autonomy. DMs complained some older supervisors (typically over 55, they noted) operated under the "my way or the highway" style of management. Many progressive companies said they weed those people out since they would not be compatible in their company's work culture at all.

SOLUTION: You most likely do not even realize you may be acting like an "old-school" manager. You may need to get some feedback from your former bosses and subordinates. Don't disregard this step — making some changes may mean the difference between holding on to your job and being next in line for a layoff, or between landing a job and remaining unemployed. DMs need executives, managers, and team members who are all open-minded, who have all learned how to evolve their already developed skills and management styles and apply them to a new and changing marketplace, noted one CEO. Many leadership courses are available to update your performance and improve your interactions with team members. Care enough to try a few and find a style that you can live with and that others under you can be productive and live with too.

What isn't tried won't work.

8. DM Concern: Less Motivation, Drive, and Energy for the Job

Many DMs stated that they had seen over-50 workers slow down significantly and perform with a lot less energy. They no longer were able to handle, nor did they want, the high-pressure jobs. DMs noted some jobs require physical stamina, with long hours, lifting, or lots of travel. Does this older man or woman have that necessary energy, many questioned, to keep up the work level of a younger person?

Depending how much over 40 the candidate was, many decision makers worried about whether the individual may have lost the drive to push hard to get the job done. They may not want to put in the extreme effort younger workers who are hungrier will. These hiring managers said they look for evidence of recent accomplishments that demonstrate the candidate still wants to get ahead. Many decision makers mentioned that, for them, the person's "drive" was a big issue, especially in people older than age 50. The over-50 worker sought to do what was necessary, but did not push for better innovations, new processes, systems, or procedures. They weren't focused on extra efforts to make important improvements to the department and organization, or even within the sphere of their own job.

They're concerned the over-40 worker wants the big paychecks, but not the actual job's demands to earn it.

SOLUTION: Energy does wane as you age. Most people do lose some zest between 40 and 60. If you do want a job that requires extra stamina, get on a fitness routine and stay with it daily. Energy drinks, vitamins, and a healthy diet will all have a positive influence on your energy.

You should take a hard look at what you want. Before you run after a new position, consider the demands, and what would be ideal for you. Maybe you can find a position where the travel is reasonable — four to five days a month as opposed to being gone twenty days every month.

You do need to prove to DMs that you are still motivated and have the drive to get the job done. You might want to explain how you have learned to enhance your already developed skills in a new and changing marketplace. For example, one DM suggested a person may have a long marketing career and be familiar with brand building through TV, radio, billboard, trade, and traditional advertising. These are solid skills that the majority of younger marketers do not have, but, as someone over 40, you need to show that you are aware of new industry trends and that your skills are relevant and applicable to them. To do this, add to your knowledge about the newer areas and learn to understand digital trends, how the Internet is specifically useful in your field, how CRM (customer relationship management) works, how social networking sites may be relevant, etc. By adding current industry knowledge to an awareness of new trends affecting your field, you can show how you can use both old methods and new to get the job done well.

One must dare to win.

9. DM Concern: Set Work Habits, Inflexibility, Not Easily Adapting to Change

Decision makers expressed concerns over older workers showing limited flexibility when it came to adapting to a new setting. They had seen older workers get too stuck doing things the way they always did them, and some put up a lot of resistance to change or growth. The older employee might be more lax about getting new training and be slower to grasp what is being taught. DMs noted, specifically in over-50 workers, that many often limit their efforts in skill development right from the start. Others pointed out that established negative patterns are accentuated as people age, and there's usually much more resistance to switching behaviors. Many workers just could not adapt to change and weren't flexible, hanging on to a "this is how we always did it" mindset.

SOLUTION: You can learn to be more modern in your approach to work. It often takes a little more effort but you can do it! Go to the bookstore and grab the three latest business books on management and productivity. Throw in a motivational book on success. Read them. They will give you new ideas to change your behavior so you can be more in sync with what employers need.

A good way to counteract this DM concern is to go online and read news about your industry, attend a conference or two, and talk to colleagues so you can give yourself a refresher course and are better able to think about trends, issues, and possible new solutions to problems an organization might be facing. You must be able to state how you might perform better in your job to make a positive contribution. You must gel with the company's pattern for job, department, division, or company improvements; make necessary productive enhancements; and continually strive to perform at a higher level.

During the job interview you'll need to offer "proof," through good examples, of your flexibility and initiative to implement change. Don't miss the important strategy in the section entitled "Show and Tell" in chapter 16.

If opportunity doesn't knock, find a door.

10. DM Concern: Expectations of Too Much Compensation or Time Off

In today's economic times the over-40 employee may bring a higher cost both in terms of salary and in benefits. Decision makers said these older executives often have inflated impressions of what they can contribute and how much they should be paid. Many decision makers said older workers seem to have an endless list of demands before taking a job. Negotiating a better deal is seen as acceptable, but unreasonable demands about vacation time, perks, and salary were a door closer.

SOLUTION: If you want top dollar, one senior VP wrote, then you'd better be able to prove with recent past accomplishments you are worth it. Keep your demands to yourself until after they offer you the job. This is where you have the most power to negotiate what you want.

You are the architect of your own future.

11. DM Concern: Overqualified for the Position

This issue launched a lot of red flags for the DMs. They worried about the "overqualified" candidate, and some said it caused them to make an automatic dismissal. Several questioned if they would be able to afford the applicant's salary and benefits expectations. Many job seekers had stressed, "I'm willing to start lower and work my way up," but this seemed like an act of desperation and an out-of-touch, dated response to the DM who heard it. Anyone who seemed desperate, willing to take "any" job, was "a major turnoff."

DMs worried that the overqualified person really wanted the DM's job and that was a major concern. If the person who was going to be the boss of the candidate was younger, the DMs wondered if the age difference would be an issue. Additionally, they worried that the candidate saw this job as temporary until he or she found a better job. Several noted that they had seen job seekers take the demotion in the past but begin asking about a promotion and start bugging the boss about a raise within a few months.

SOLUTION: The simplest and wisest solution is to look harder for positions you *are qualified for.* There may be fewer opportunities, but you can spend your time putting maximum effort into locating these positions that fit your level of expertise and experience.

If you still want to look lower, you may need to make some resume revisions that pull out or at the very least tone down some of the higher skills and accomplishments. It's not uncommon for job seekers with PhDs to remove this degree from their resume because DMs label them as too academic for jobs outside of the field of education.

Decision makers want you to have a valid reason for being willing to take a step down. Acceptable rationales include wanting to change industries, preferring a job with fewer management demands, wanting to travel less, and needing greater job satisfaction. Some may be attracted to the new organization's products or a humanitarian cause.

You'll find solid strategies in chapters 11, 12, and 13 on resume creation, and chapter 17, "Acing the Job Interview," on how to counteract this objection/concern.

> Struggles you face today are the price
> you pay for victory tomorrow.

12. DM Concern: Thinking the Old Way Is the Best Way

Several decision makers stated that the greatest mistake an over-40 individual can make is to believe that tried and true is always best. This is particularly worrisome if the person has been with only one or two companies throughout his or her career yet still feels that the way the old company did things was the "right" or "best" way. It came across in interviews and it was a big turnoff.

SOLUTION: One top executive explained a solution pretty clearly, saying, "Many executives, managers, and professionals have been brainwashed to believe that 'the Xerox way was best,' or 'at Motorola we did it like this,' etc. Individuals over 40 need to realize that there are many different approaches that can be successful to driving business and they have to, in some sense, let go of the past and bring their relevant skills to the table." Another company president made this point: "I have always sought out diversity in backgrounds of my managers to make up a mix of opinions and skills. Too many corporations want to have cloned employees and they then only get yes-men, which can lead to serious problems if the economy or industry goes into a downward spiral."

Perhaps it's time for some refresher courses on new leadership styles and more creative problem-solving techniques. Additionally, you may have great ideas you can bring from your former company's systems, processes, or procedures, but be sure to stress in interviews you are open to learning how *they* operate. You can mention that you often look to uncover better ways to get results by blending the best parts of both.

If you are going to be in a position of leadership, you are expected to encourage everyone on the team, or within the company, to reach goals and deliver solutions to company problems. Demonstrating during your interview that you are open-minded by giving an example or two of successful collaboration will negate this concern.

STRATEGY

To briefly summarize how to counteract their concerns:

- Sell *results.*
- Show up enthused, vibrant, and excited.
- Make sure your appearance is up-to-date; hire a makeover expert if needed.
- Be prepared to go back to school if your computer and technical skills are out-of-date.
- Be willing to work for someone younger than you.
- Understand how to motivate and work with a younger workforce.
- Be prepared to prove your stamina and drive to the employer.
- Do not act "old school."
- Package yourself as a winner.
- Make sure you address the overqualified issue correctly.

Many of the twelve concerns will quickly fall by the wayside if you focus your resume, cover letters, and interview conversations to sell the results you've achieved in your last few jobs.

We can all get discouraged when an employer doesn't hire us. We can get angry, bitter, and even scream, "What do they want?" That frustration will just bring you down if you dwell on it. Rejection will happen. But so will success. You are capable of changing and reinventing yourself. Look in the mirror and say, "Tomorrow I am going to be better than I am today," then list five action steps to make that happen and *do them* right away.

You create your own future. Strive to make yours better than it was in the past.

■ ■ ■ ■

PART 2
THE HIDDEN
JOB MARKET

■ ■ ■ ■

"If you want your life to be a magnificent
story, realize you are the author.
Each day you have the opportunity
to write a new page."

ROBIN RYAN

CHAPTER 4
FINDING
UNADVERTISED JOBS

"Little goals deliver small achievements,
but big goals get you greater rewards."
ROBIN RYAN

Most job openings — about 80% — are
never publicly advertised, yet this hidden
job market is where you'll find the best jobs.
This is where you are going to concentrate
your job search.

It's important to understand the hiring
process in order to recognize the best ways
to penetrate the hidden job market. Let's
consider an example of what happens inside
an organization large enough to have a human resources department.

Sara is the product manager at a large
high-tech company. One of her employees
has resigned this morning, leaving Sara with
an opening for a project manager. Her first
thought is to review those she knows within
her department and determine who among

them could handle the job. She then checks her files for anyone who has recently written or called her. If none come to mind, she immediately goes to the other people on her team and those who work in her division, to see if they might know of someone qualified to fill the opening.

Sara recognizes that a referral from her staff is an excellent way to find a good technical project manager. If this effort doesn't yield any prospects, however, Sara emails her colleagues, other managers at different companies, explains she has an opening, and asks for referrals. She may contact a professional association to make it aware of this opening. Perhaps the association staff can refer someone within their membership. If these efforts do not yield any prime candidates, her next approach might be to inform all the employees within her company of the new opening, using an internal email or by posting it on the company's intranet, which is viewed only by employees.

Sara is willing to go to a lot of effort to find a replacement before approaching the human resources office. She believes that from her network she'll get referrals that will produce a better employee than general recruiting techniques, such as online ads or recruiting firms. Furthermore, Sara knows she's apt to find a qualified candidate more quickly in the hidden job market. Sara will also be on the lookout for any resumes referred to her even after human resources staff have taken over the search.

This hiring manager is well aware that turning the process over to the company's human resources department initiates a two- to three-month effort. It takes time for advertising, recruiting, and screening hundred of applicants, in order to select a few people to interview. During this process, Sara knows that she will be overworked: the opening leaves a gap that she and her staff will have to fill. There will be overtime and the risk of falling behind on some projects. Sara chooses to exhaust the unadvertised, hidden job market to substantially shorten the hiring process.

Like Sara, many other decision makers have repeatedly stated that the best employees are uncovered using the referral process. In additional, some new jobs are only known to the decision maker. Perhaps he or she is thinking about replacing someone or knows a member of the team is leaving, either for personal reasons or because of a promotion. The manager may be aware of upcoming staffing needs, unannounced projects, or departmental expansions, as well as impending retirements. He or she may also be reacting to challenging business situations the organization is facing. In other words, the executives or managers will soon have a need that you may be able to fill, even if they are still in the planning stage. You must find these decision makers. They aren't looking to find you — yet. They will be open-minded and quite interested when they are offered talent they can use to meet these anticipated needs. And, at this point, there is no competition standing on the sidelines eager to push you out of the way.

THE PROCESS

You can enter the hidden job market by using four basic techniques:

- Researching the job market for leads.
- Cultivating your network and asking for referrals.
- Scheduling informational interviews.
- Writing effective prospecting letters.

Your goal at this point is to obtain detailed information about the company's operations and organizational structure, develop leads to people inside the organization, and learn the names and titles of company administrators and their bosses.

We are purposely skirting around human resource administrators, although they likely hold a key to the names of the contacts you will need. You need to attempt to make direct contact with *the person who has the need for a new employee,* the "boss" with the power to hire. Unless you have personal friends in the human resources department, they aren't likely to put a lot of effort into helping you. Their job is to screen applicants and that typically means being a good gatekeeper — and screening you out.

Discovering potential positions for which you are qualified, within the hidden job market, allows you to meet directly with hiring managers and learn from them what their hiring needs are, without hundreds of others vying for the same job.

Using the techniques we are going to talk about will change the traditional ways of job hunting you have used in the past. You may question the process at first because it is time-consuming and the benefits are not immediately evident. These techniques take effort, planning, and organization. You must make a commitment to be proactive in conducting research. You need to be assertive in contacting potential employers, setting up appointments, asking acquaintances for help, and actively meeting people. If you are shy and introverted, you may have some difficulty at first, but with practice, using the specific techniques outlined in the next couple of chapters, you will find it easier to make the contacts necessary to find a really good job.

PROSPECTING LETTERS, COLD-CALLING, AND DIRECT MAIL

Some authors, career counselors, and on-line services see direct mail and cold-calling employers as *the* way to land a job. They advise you to mail out hundreds (sometimes thousands) of resumes — usually to employers you find on an address list that you purchase directly from the author, career counselor, or online service. They tout this as the only great way to land a good job. I disagree for these reasons:

- Only a small few have had success using mass mailing campaigns. This approach is an enormous amount of work, with many suggesting you do ten to fifteen follow-up calls a day.
- It takes dozens of hours of research to find the decision maker's name.
- The rejection rate is gigantic.

Until I see positive results from dozens of

people using this method — and to date I haven't seen more than three or four — I do not recommend it. I also asked decision makers at middle levels and up, including C-level executives, and almost all said they just throw out unsolicited letters. Unless it comes from a source they know, it goes in the trash. Maybe a time or two someone did get lucky and the right resume found the right person at the right time, when there was a need, but about 98% of the time, straight cold-calling doesn't work. Concentrate on developing a referral network and making a connection first before you write to a decision maker. It's a much better, more effective door opener.

CHAPTER 5
FINDING
POTENTIAL EMPLOYERS

"Do it *now.*
Today will be yesterday tomorrow."
ROBIN RYAN

The purpose of job market research is to uncover leads on potential positions, get information on specific companies, find names of prospective employers, locate sources of information on jobs, learn about industry trends, and identify resources that can aid you in your job hunt. Market research can be done on the Internet, at the local library, over the telephone, and in conversations with colleagues, associates, and friends. You can do your job market research anywhere and everywhere. Standing in the checkout line at a grocery store, watching your kid's sporting event with other parents — pretty much at any time or place the opportunity presents itself. It's up to you to take the initiative. Ask the person sitting next to you at the baseball game where he or she works; ask questions about the company, who runs the department you'd likely work in, if he or she knows of any openings that might fit your qualifications. Help is everywhere if you actively look for it.

GET HELP FROM YOUR LOCAL LIBRARY

Abundant sources of information exist, and maybe starting on the Internet makes sense to you, but in fact, you will save time if you start at the library. A reference librarian can be indispensable in your search.

A reference librarian is the over-40 job hunter's new best friend. This person has access to a wealth of information, particularly on local employers. Librarians know about specialty or little-known job listings, job search websites, and databases that offer employer information you cannot access anywhere else. Stop by your local library and introduce yourself to the librarian. Ask where the reference materials on job searching are located. Your librarian can show you where to find information about local companies, point out business directories, and locate company publications. Sometimes just a phone call can get you more information about specific companies that are hiring, a name and address, even a phone number that will lead you in the right direction.

I have taught many job search seminars at libraries in the Seattle suburbs, and I have seen the reference materials these libraries can offer people who are looking for work. Not only can you get individual help from librarians, but they offer other resources such as free computer classes and job search seminars.

Your detective skills, along with the help of a librarian, will enable you to gather information so you will be able to:

- Create a list of employers that especially interest you.
- Research the names and titles of the managers who run these companies or departments.

Here are some ideas that will help you accomplish your research:

- Target companies of interest by looking at local business journals, the business section of newspapers, and industry magazines.
- Search geographically, identifying specific cities, towns, regions, and

states where you would be willing to live and work.

- Review local job listings to identify companies and organizations that are advertising for and hiring new people.

Most libraries subscribe to many business directories and databases. The reference librarian will be able to assist you in locating these resources.

Business libraries, especially those located in major universities, are excellent sources of business information and usually are open to the public. You will be amazed at the speedy access to information that these business libraries can offer.

Here are a few good resources to check out and to use at the library:

- **REFERENCE USA** — a large database full of companies and fields, searchable by location, names of key executives, etc.
- **ASSOCIATIONS UNLIMITED** — allows you to look for local chapters and conferences in your field or industry.
- **HOOVER'S** — lists U.S. companies, sales volumes, number of employees, company decision makers and officers.
- **PLUNKETT RESEARCH** — lists compa-

nies by industry.

SEARCHING THE INTERNET

Online you will find some useful information to help you create a list of prospective employers. For example: Google your field, adding the word "jobs" after it, such as: "communications jobs" or "civil engineering jobs."

You'll find some great resources fast using this shortcut.

Some of the better online resources to find corporate information that can be useful to uncover job leads includes:

- Search engines — e.g., WWW.GOOGLE.COM.
- WWW.HOOVERS.COM — great information — free information through most libraries; this site charges a fee for most individual use.
- WWW.VAULT.COM — some free information — nice listings by industry; some detailed company profiles require a fee to access.
- WWW.BIZJOURNALS.COM — access to city business journals for free.
- WWW.INDUSTRYWEEK.COM — lists the one thousand largest manufacturers, with snapshot information.

- WWW.INVESTORCALENDAR.COM — links to annual reports for large and midsize companies.
- WWW.BBB.ORG/US/CHARITY — detailed and comprehensive listing of nonprofits.

WHAT TO LOOK FOR

The kind of information you are seeking includes names, addresses, phone numbers, and lists of companies or organizations. Your sources are trade journals, business directories, newspapers, magazines, even the Yellow Pages. Check company publications to see if they list new products, services, business developments, and growth plans for the next few years. Pay attention when reading business journals or newspapers. Whenever you read about a new store opening or a nonprofit's special event or a company expanding into a new service area, it is fair to draw the conclusion that this means new jobs. Make note of any organization that might need your kind of expertise. Include information such as company size, growth potential, names of managers, anything that might help you make contact with a decision maker on the inside of the company.

REVIEW THE COMPANY'S WEBSITE

Any company that is publicly traded on the stock market has an annual report, which will most likely be available to read on the company's website. If you can't find it, call the investor relations department or email that division and ask that their annual report be sent to you. Annual reports contain valuable information on company growth, new products and services, new regional offices that are planned, and the names of top management.

Review the website to learn more about what the company does. You must know the general facts, such as who might own the company (many large companies, like Kraft Foods, have a lot of brands under their umbrella). As you investigate look to see who might be expanding, who is moving divisions, or who has the job type you seek. These usually mean job openings are coming available. Delve into the website and you can often find a list of contacts: names and titles. They are often buried deep in the layers of website pages, but many times they are there.

TIP: To save some time, at the bottom of any company's home page look for a reference to a "Site Map." This can prove to be a shortcut, enabling you to quickly find the information you want.

USE THE PEOPLE METHOD

Most people work for smaller companies, those with fewer than one thousand employees. These employers are harder — but not impossible — to research. One very effective way is to ask other people in your network about companies they work for. *What does the company do? Does it employ any people who perform the job you are seeking?* Be sure you are specific about the job title you are qualified to perform, and identify the department you are interested in. For example: "I am looking for work as a marketing communication executive and have twenty years of experience working in large companies." Do not use any jargon, such as "I'm in mar com," as the person you are asking may be unfamiliar with that term. Being specific is the best way to get names of both decision makers and new potential contacts within a company.

Good detectives begin with what they know, so start making a list that addresses these questions:

- Who can I ask for information in my field?
- Who else would know people perform-

ing the job I want to do?

- Who knows someone at one or more of the companies on my list?
- Who has industry knowledge? (The best resource is often officers in professional or trade associations; i.e., CPA societies for accountants, union organizations for engineers, college associations for administrators, etc.).

Keep a comprehensive list of the people who help you so you'll know who told you about a specific company, or who gave you a certain contact's name. This list is a gold mine as you continue to plow through your market research.

PROFESSIONAL ASSOCIATIONS

Members of professional associations are great sources of information and new contacts. These organizations often have a directory or website that lists member companies or groups. You can make contacts by attending their meetings or one of their conferences. The Internet contains lists of conferences and trade shows by region, industry, and occupation. It will alert you to meetings related to your field of interest. To find a trade association in any field, say, a meeting planners association, go online and Google "meeting planners association"; this should produce a list for you. Another resource the library offers is the Encyclopedia of Associations, a directory of U.S. organizations.

A trade association can provide excellent career information about its field, the types of jobs available, salary ranges, where people are getting hired, trends, and announcements of future plans. Association newsletters often have articles about people in the profession, and they help keep you up-to-date on current jargon. For example, an accountant working in the computer software industry might wish to make a career change to hospital administration. He would need to conduct extensive market research, perhaps joining one of these associations, to expand his knowledge of the special skills an accountant might need in the field of hospital accounting systems, such as third-party billing. Consider setting up informational interviews with association officers. They are valuable contacts and usually willing to talk to people interested in their field.

STUDY TRENDS IN YOUR INDUSTRY

If you are a member of the over-40 club, prospective employers stated they are concerned that you may be out of touch, can't learn new technology, or are content to rest on your laurels and won't be a productive employee. To overcome these perceptions you must be right on top of what is going on in your field or industry. You must be eager to participate in new projects, and you must be prepared for new challenges. The research you do prior to accepting a new position will certainly update you about changes, trends, and anything new in your industry.

Take time to read the last six to eight months' worth of business journals in your field, plus any kind of magazine articles that come to your attention. Go online and read blogs, recent articles, and industry news. Be sure to check the source; many that you find online aren't completely accurate. Read the economic news in your local newspaper. Pay attention to announcements of new developments and business opportunities.

A valuable result comes from all this effort and all this research: it will make you more successful in all communications with potential employers, and with your new boss.

SUMMARY

You won't find a directory or article with the title "New Job Openings from the Hidden Job Market." You will need to sharpen your detective skills, spend some time in the library, and read professional journals to gain insight and information on potential employers.

Start creating your list today! Develop a list of thirty potential employers. Why thirty? More often than not, job hunters have only one or two prospects going at any one time, and when these possibilities fail, it can be debilitating. Knowing you have ten or even twenty other opportunities that may prove advantageous will soften the blow when one turns out to be a dead end or you are turned down for that position you were counting on.

Job market research is not something you do only once and forget. It is an ongoing effort you must use throughout your job search. If you run out of leads, go back to the library and continue your research. Plow through magazines, trade journals, the Yellow Pages, newspapers. Locate and attend association meetings. Continue to add to your market research, to explore more companies, to look for more contacts with people who can help make your job search effective. You will be amazed at the number of opportunities and possibilities you never knew existed.

For the most current list of my favorite online resources, and some download-able forms to help make finding prospective employers easier, go to WWW .ROBINRYAN.COM/BOOKREADER.

CHAPTER 6
REFERRAL
NETWORKING

"Be so good they won't ignore you."
ROBIN RYAN

You know people who know people — who know more people. These can be very helpful to your job search — or you can waste your lifetime's worth of networking contacts and let a terrific job pass you by. Think about it this way: if employers don't know about you, they can't hire you.

Referral networking is meeting people and asking very specific questions on:

- Companies you are interested in
- Anyone they know who works inside these organizations
- People already performing your exact type of job
- Who the hiring manager/decision maker is

121

SUCCESS RATES

The U.S. Department of Labor each year produces a list of statistics on job search techniques. Among its recent findings:

- The success rate from job hunting online is 4%, up from 2% a few years ago.
- The success rate from utilizing contacts to find a job is 63%.

Using contacts you have — and those you get to know — has been the most successful technique over the last decade. That is how two-thirds of all jobs are found! Therefore make networking your top job search technique. It's the strategy you should spend the most time utilizing.

Your ultimate goal is to use contacts in a very effective way to apply for a new job. This includes doing some informational interviews and connecting with other people to expand your contacts, ultimately to reach decision makers.

FINDING CONTACTS

Begin with who you know. The nice thing about being over 40 is you know a lot of people. Create your list, including:

- Friends — current and old

- Relatives
- Neighbors
- Social acquaintances and their spouses
- Former bosses
- Colleagues
- Former coworkers
- Former employees you have supervised
- Vendors (company contacts) you've done business with
- Service people (librarians, business editors, career counselors, teachers, politicians, etc.)
- Association officers
- College alumni
- People from your church or social club

Start with those you know well. But have a tactical plan *before* you contact anyone.

INFORMATIONAL INTERVIEWING

This is a two-step process, and the technique is designed to learn about a company, its work culture, and your prospective job duties, and to find the name of the person who could hire you. You actually set up an interview, usually through a personal referral, and you ask the person to spend fifteen to twenty minutes advising you on your job search. You are up-front in your request but always reassure the person you are approaching that you don't expect him to know of a job or have a job for you. You do state that he could be very helpful by merely sharing information. It's important to be honest. Simply say, "You could help me with my career direction," or "I could use your advice," or "I desire information on your field, your industry, your geographical area, your company." Stress that you only want fifteen to twenty minutes maximum.

This tool will allow you to directly contact hiring managers — eventually. Most people do not start at the top because they don't know who the decision maker is, since that name is not always easy to find.

Begin by using your network. Start with those that you are very familiar with. Ask anyone you talk to if they know of any person who works in the organizations you are interested in. From that inside person, you can uncover the organizational structure, learn about the company in depth, find out about any new products or services being offered, and get the decision maker's name. You may even discover if the company has — or will soon have — a job opening you'd qualify for. If they aren't hiring anytime soon, you could share the list of other companies you have identified that you would like to work for from your prospect list and ask them:

1. Do they know anyone who works at any of these organizations?
2. Can they think of any other companies (especially smaller ones) that you should consider?

You will learn a lot of valuable information that will be helpful in your job search. You ask the questions; you control where the conversation goes. This conversation can greatly aid you in learning what is needed, what skills they want, and where the company (and, if you're changing fields, the industry) is headed.

You will also learn which transferable skills you already possess that the employer will value. And if they require a skill you don't have, then you need to learn it, take a class, or consider a different opportunity.

In time, through these interviews, you will get names of the people who have the power to hire you in the organizations where you wish to work. Make your request by phone or email, and be sure you state the name of the person who is referring you.

Most informational interviews are done on the phone, but on rare occasions you may meet at the person's office or for lunch.

Try to avoid email since it doesn't allow for the give-and-take that extensive questions require; but for a quick question or two, email may be a viable way to conduct a brief interview and get a lead. Be sure you prepare for the interview by reading the organization's literature. Write out your questions and prioritize them since you may only get to have a few answered.

Prepare questions such as *What are the major responsibilities required in performing this job? What are some of the traits necessary to succeed on the job?* You might ask detailed questions about the company organization or structure. Start your informational interview by taking sixty seconds to reintroduce yourself, mention the referring person's name, and explain your reason for calling. This will save time and allow you to ask specific questions and get answers in the time allotted. You might talk about trends in the field, procedures, products, programs, or new business developments. You direct the questioning to elicit answers that will help you understand the job and the employer's needs. Take notes.

Always ask for new referrals. Inquire about any other people the person can think of that you should meet who could help you. This keeps your networking efforts going and eventually you'll begin to meet the decision makers. At the end of fifteen or twenty minutes, whether you're finished or not, thank the person for his or her time, explain that you recognize his or her time is valuable, express how helpful the interview has been for you, and hang up. Yes, end the call. It's critical that you do not abuse the time that the person has generously given you.

In a perfect world, every contact would open his or her door and offer wonderful job leads. Don't count on it, but it does happen. Realize this is a long process, as some interviews will connect you to very helpful people, and some will be a dud.

Immediately after you are finished with the interview take a few minutes to write down your impressions about the person and the organization. Do send a handwritten thank-you note, which is more impressive than an email and therefore much more preferable. Be sure to add your business card inside. No business card? Then create one on your computer or have inexpensive ones printed — a great resource we use a lot is www.qualidee.com. Be sure your name, address, home phone, and email address are on the cards, along with a job title that you are looking for. Have a stack for any events or meetings you go to and give them out freely.

Informational interviewing is a terrific tool to learn about new fields and different jobs, uncover job openings, and find out the exact skills employers value and hire for.

Several clients, especially top executives, have reported that this approach worked very well. You'll learn firsthand about an employer's needs, and now that you are acquainted, it often gets you an "in" to send your resume directly to this hiring manager.

The second step in using the informational interviewing techniques is to meet and talk to the decision maker.

MEETING THE DECISION MAKER

When you learn of an opening — say you see a position listed on a website — your first step is to search your contacts (and their contacts) and try to uncover the name of someone who works inside that specific organization. If you find someone, then you can approach the contact with a simple request: *can you please forward my resume on to the hiring manager?* This is your first choice. If your contact doesn't know who that is, and neither do you, then make your second-choice request: *please send my resume, via company email or intranet, to the human resource manager.* Either way, you will have moved your application documents to the top of the pile and stand a greater chance of securing an interview.

You'll have much more success if you approach any contact with a specific request, such as "Do you know anyone who works at Wells Fargo Bank?" This specific request has two possible answers: no, or — *bingo* — yes, I do. Then ask for the name and contact info. *It does not matter what job that person holds* at the bank. Any insider can look up who might supervise the area you are looking into. Why would this stranger help you? Often it's because of the connection — you are members of the same college or group, or she knows the person who sent you to her. It may actually be a friend or former coworker and she is happy to help if she can.

So you can better understand how this process works, here is an example. A client recently saw her dream job at Goldman Sachs. Although she had no direct Wall Street experience, she did have a distinctive skill set to qualify for this specific job. She used all her contacts, but no one knew anyone inside this company. I suggested she try her college's MBA alumni to see who was at Goldman. She found two very senior executives and decided to approach one with this request. It was simple and direct — summarizing her experience and linking their college connection. She asked for the recipient's help to forward on her application. Mind you, this client did not know this executive, and the exec did not know her.

A simple email came back saying: "I forwarded it on . . . good luck." Moral of the story: finding a connection and getting a referral's help can truly open doors.

GUIDELINES

1. **BE VERY SPECIFIC.** The clearer you are on the type of help you want and the exact job title you are seeking, the better assistance you'll get from anyone you network with.
2. **ASK FOR WHAT YOU WANT.** Many decision makers, managers, and colleagues know job hunting is no fun. And many have been in your shoes before so be clear and simply state your request. If it's to determine growth areas of business or learn what skills are needed to change careers say so.
3. **ASK FOR LEADS AND INTRODUC-**

TIONS. Go through your list of prospective employers. Ask the contacts if they know anybody who works or has worked for the companies that are on your list. Do they know of any other companies not on the list that you should include as prospects? Any vendors who sell supplies to those companies? Someone who works for similar companies on the list? Also ask if they know of anyone who's doing the job that you're looking for. By asking your network for specific suggestions, you'll get specific answers. Networking is far from a new concept. Many over-40 job hunters in the past used networking by asking a contact, "Do you know about a job?" The answer often would be "No." The strategy outlined above will identify excellent leads to get you inside information about companies you might never have been exposed to. The help you get from friends and acquaintances with this strategy may turn you on to some people who can eventually produce a job lead for you!

4. **REASSURE THEM.** State right up

front, "I'm looking for a new job as a [fill in the blank with your job title]. I don't expect you to have a job opening, but I sure could use some help and information." This approach will get you a lot more assistance than if they think you are just hitting on them for a job.

5. **BE RESPECTFUL OF THEIR TIME.** Asking a few questions or sending a couple of emails requesting quick responses are the best ways to get help, win friends, and avoid being viewed as a pest.

6. **SAY THANK YOU** — handwritten notes are best.

CHAPTER 7
FINDING JOB OPENINGS USING WEBSITES AND ONLINE JOB BOARDS

"Every accomplishment big or small
starts with the decision to try."

ROBIN RYAN

Looking online can uncover many job openings. You will want to use this resource to find them. Combining this with the referral networking tools discussed in chapter 6 will greatly enhance your success since a posted listing often brings in many, many applicants.

Regardless of which websites you use, you need to detail three specific things before beginning your online search:

- The precise job title of the position you are seeking
- Effective keywords to search on
- Location — city, state, or region — you are interested in

Save yourself a great deal of time. Begin by reviewing the websites of the thirty companies you've identified where you would be interested in working.

Next go to niche sites. Many are free. These are specific for a field or industry. Most are sponsored by a professional association. For example, a human resource manager would look for her own job at WWW.SHRM.ORG, which has HR industry listings. A six-figure executive could try his industry websites, or those focused on executives who earn over $100,000 per year, like WWW.THELADDERS.COM.

Some job listing services charge a fee. Some are worth the money; some are not. Check to see if they have a free trial or a sample to see if they list enough openings in your geographical region, and under your job title, to make the investment worthwhile. Be cautious. Use a credit card to pay for these services, not a debit card or cash. A credit card offers more protection, as in refunds, in case you are dissatisfied with the advertised service. Ask friends if they used it and if it was worth the investment. The costs vary, but a subscription to a job listing service is typically about $20 to $40 per month. Also check to determine where the postings on a given listing site originate. How old are they? Investigate how often the listing service updates, if it frequently removes old or filled positions, if it adds new ones daily, etc. If the information is not kept up-to-date, the site will likely waste too much of your time.

DON'T RELY ON EMAIL ALERTS

When you use job boards, they often let you save your resume and cover letters. This is a convenience and a time saver.

Many listing sites suggest you sign up for email alerts, so you can be notified whenever a new job with your noted job field gets posted by an employer. The problem is that these mechanisms don't work very well. If you use them, you could be losing out on numerous positions on this listing board website. When I've worked with clients and we searched these sites together, each client expressed surprise to see positions that would fit, even though they never received an email notice about these job openings.

BEST STRATEGY: Bookmark several job boards and visit them often, searching them yourself. Realize that all sites have filters so try various job titles to be sure you don't miss openings.

SWEEP SITES

A sweep site scours the Internet to find job openings listed on large company websites or paid websites, online newspaper listings, some niche sites, etc. Sounds like a dream world, right? Nope! The filters are few, so you end up looking at a lot of listings before you find something you are truly interested in. These sites require good keywords to make them useful. When using a sweep site as a resource, plan on devoting a lot of hours to the search. While I do use them with clients, given a choice, company websites are my first choice, followed by specific job title/industry niche sites.

Two particularly good sweep sites, as I write this, are WWW.INDEED.COM and WWW.SIMPLYHIRED.COM. Since websites come and go quickly, find the most current recommendations on my website, at WWW.ROBINRYAN.COM/BOOKREADER.

STRATEGY

The biggest negative to looking on Internet job boards or websites is that no computer is going to hire you. The computer does not react to your cover letter and resume; it doesn't interview you — only real human beings do that. Use your time wisely. Spend a set number of hours online, and spend even more hours *connecting and talking to real people*. Networking or meeting with employers is the key. Not doing this is a big mistake.

GENERAL RULES FOR RESPONDING ONLINE

No matter what your job level, you must learn how to search websites and how to respond and apply online. Employers will ask you either to attach your resume to an email or paste it into their online application. These tasks are second nature to some over-40 applicants and seem to be impossible technical challenges to others. Still, you *must* learn and master them.

Guidelines for applying online:
- Be certain the format you use to prepare your cover letter and resume can be read on the receiving end of the transmission. Home computers often come preloaded with simple word processing systems, but it is often incompatible with what employers use. Just about all companies use Microsoft

Word; therefore, *make sure* that you are using MS Word software to create all the resumes and cover letters you may need to submit electronically.

- Follow the employer's directions carefully. Some request that you attach your cover letter and resume; while some still prefer that you copy and paste your materials directly into the body of your email. This likely will need some reformatting to make it look okay. Be sure it's looking acceptable before you hit "Send."

- If you aren't instructed to do otherwise, instead of attaching a file, it is much more effective to paste your cover letter and resume *inside* the email. Companies often run filters on attachments but not so much on email. So this dramatically improves the chances the recipient will actually get your resume and cover letter.

- Whenever possible, email only one file. Just create a single document with your cover letter as page 1; and then your resume immediately following as pages 2 (and 3). Save them as a single file, not two separate files. This better ensures that both documents (in the one file) get through together.

Consider Using a PDF File

More and more employers are moving away from MS Word attachments due to viruses the files might contain. Sending documents through cyberspace can cause changes in the fonts and style of your resume and cover letter — small irregularities or more significant shifting. If the employer is able to receive attached files, converting your documents to a PDF file will eliminate style and formatting problems. Check out free PDF creators online by searching "create PDF." Once you have generated a PDF file, you can't alter it, so proofread, proofread, proofread, and finalize edits and changes before you convert your original file to PDF format. This is a smart way to send your resume and cover letter.

Send a Second Copy via U.S. Postal Service

It's been estimated that about one-third of all resumes sent electronically on the Internet cannot be read due to some technical snafu. Cover your bases and mail a copy to the prospective employer from your local post office. Address it to the hiring manager, if you have a name, or to the human resources department. Few applicants take this extra step and it can be important. A real person still opens the mail; someone will surely glance at it, whereas online a real person may never lay eyes on it. Why? Big companies often receive 2,000 resumes a day; some average 100,000 electronically submitted resumes per month. This follow-up postal mail procedure can double your chances. If you are missed in the company's electronic keyword search, which examines incoming resumes to automatically sort them, you'll at least be seen when someone opens the mail. To get your resume noticed, you must stand out from the crowd, but many large companies require submission electronically so submitting both ways covers all your bases.

SPECIFIC TIPS WHEN APPLYING ONLINE

- **USE THE EMAIL SUBJECT LINE TO IDENTIFY THE TYPE OF JOB YOU ARE APPLYING FOR.** Include the job code, if one is listed in the posting. For example, "Subject: Marketing Manager, #71675." This is the key to helping the recipient "sort" your application or forward it to the correct internal hiring manager.
- **SEND YOUR MATERIALS FROM THE COMPANY'S OWN WEBSITE IF POSSIBLE.** Many larger job listings ask you

to use their online "Apply" button. Always check to see if the job opening is available on the company's own website, and if so, go there to apply through the company site. It is a better and more direct process.

- **PUT YOUR NAME PROMINENTLY IN THE RESUME FILE NAME.** Always save your resume and cover letter using your first and last name so the file name would be, for example, "Tom Norton resume.doc." This allows for easier retrieval and sorting by the recipient.

- **EMAIL FROM YOUR HOME COMPUTER.** Current employers can and often do review employees' computers and check their email and online searches. So stay out of trouble and keep your resumes and online applications only on your own home or personal computer.

- **FORGET RESUME BLASTING.** This service is a waste of your dollars, and employers *hate* getting unsolicited resume blasts. These services offer to send your resume electronically to hundreds of employers. This sounds promising, but it's all hype and won't find you a job, so simply don't do it!

- **POSTING YOUR RESUME.** There are pros: *maybe a recruiter will see you;* but there are a lot of cons to posting your resume. Very few recruiters (with the exception of some high-tech in-house HR recruiters) scour the Internet looking for resumes online. Employers do want good talent, but most aren't sophisticated enough to use this method effectively, nor do they have the time to search that hard for you. I've never had a client or job search seminar attendee ever land a job from posting their resume online. In fact, posting it can cause you unseen problems. Your name, address, email, and phone number are now available to every spammer out there. And if you are already employed, what if your company or your boss sees the posting? Are you prepared for those consequences? Electronic postings can last a long, long time. Consider carefully before you do it. I don't recommend it at all. The exceptions are professional association sites and a business network site like LinkedIn.

WHERE NOT TO GO

Monster.com is the best-known job board. The company has spent millions of dollars on getting the brand name recognized. It may be the only job board you have heard of. In my opinion, it is one of the least effective places to spend any time looking for a job when you are over 40. It caters to the more entry-level job seekers, and it has many old listings, as well as ghost jobs (not real jobs, just people wanting to capture your email address for the purpose of marketing something else to you). When you are over 40, checking this site is not worth your time.

SUMMARY: GOOD WEBSITES TO USE

I can tell you that there are many good websites you can use. These sites change so frequently that any list I write today will surely be different in sixty days. Since I'm online a lot with clients, I stay on top of the better ones to use. And clients also alert me to any especially good ones in their field. So every month I update my recommendations on my website to save you time. Get the most current list of websites offering job openings by going to my website: WWW.ROBINRYAN.COM/BOOKREADER.

CHAPTER 8
JOB HUNTING ON
SOCIAL NETWORKS

"You lose out on 100% of the opportunities that you never go after."

ROBIN RYAN

Do not confuse the social networks the under-30 crowd uses with a business professional network. You want business contacts, and sites like Facebook are not the place to start creating those. Two options work — and work very well — for anyone over 40: LinkedIn and your college alumni network.

LINKEDIN

The best social networking site devoted to business relationships and full of potential contacts is LinkedIn (WWW.LINKEDIN .COM). This site has millions of members from around the globe. Likely someone you know is on it: certainly former bosses and coworkers and former schoolmates are likely to be members.

144

Microsoft's senior recruiting director offered this insight: "You should have a profile on LinkedIn. This is a great resource for outreach and finding people who work at companies you want to apply to. It's ideal to search out former bosses, coworkers, and colleagues. It's also a place where higher-end jobs are posted with direct access to the hiring manager or recruiter. You can network here to get good insider information. That invaluable insight will help you excel if you get an interview."

If you are wondering how good this resource is, it has gotten much better recently. A client told me about her experience. Jo had been out of the IT world for about eight years. She wanted to return to work so she began trying to find a new job. I suggested she look up old colleagues and connect with anyone she could find from the old companies she had worked for. She stated that she'd been a lousy networker and had lost touch, too preoccupied with her kids and traveling. Although she'd joined LinkedIn, she hadn't used it yet. We started searching her old company on LinkedIn. She found two colleagues and her old boss. He was thrilled to hear from Jo and they set up a phone chat. Under his guidance, she returned to college for a couple of tech refresher courses, and he planned to hire her back as soon as she finished. This is how Jo got hired. It demonstrates the power of networking, especially if your former colleague holds you in high esteem.

LinkedIn has a few more positive uses:

1. You can search your network to find someone with a contact who works at a company you are applying to. Then you can try to make a connection with that person directly. Once you do that, request his or her help in sending your resume through the company's internal system to HR or the hiring manager, as this significantly ups your chances of getting noticed.

2. The "People" search feature on LinkedIn is helpful; use HR and recruiters plus the company you want to try to get hired with. For example, typing "Apple recruiter" into the keyword search for people turned up almost one thousand people.

3. Searching under "Companies" will give you a wealth of information. When I selected an industry, "publishing," I found 2,718 companies

listed. From there, I clicked and got a comprehensive snapshot of employees and former employees, data on company size, business revenues, etc. It also alerted me to people already in my network who know someone in that organization. It's a very helpful tool — it takes some time, but it's a great way to network.

4. Create your own profile and list the colleges you went to. Then you can look for former classmates. You can also search on the college itself. I searched on Boston College, my alma mater, and found 56,370 people listed who attended this university — a pretty amazing use of technology that can be a new tool to help you find those unadvertised jobs.

5. Look under the "Jobs" tab and you'll see middle management up to C-level positions posted. They have the direct contact, so you can respond to the HR manager, recruiter, or DM who posted the opening.

COLLEGE NETWORKS
ARE A GOLD MINE

You have absolutely nothing in common with 99% of all the alumni who graduated from your university except one key thing — the college. And that is an instant door opener to conversations. Today most colleges and universities have an alumni office that offers email connections to any past graduate. Graduate programs such as law schools and MBA programs usually have specialized career alumni groups already set up to put you in contact with others who have said they'd help alums in their job search. This is a *great* resource many people don't know about. For example, Bob, an engineer who wanted to move into international marketing, went to grad school at night to earn his MBA. Once he completed the degree, he spent three years exploring internal opportunities in search of landing a promotion. Frustrated that it didn't happen, he decided to job hunt and find a better advancement opportunity for himself somewhere else. I suggested this client tap his college network and he indeed found two people at the company he had his eye on — Chevron. Neither was in his field, but an email introduction, followed by a phone call, had the first man agreeing to forward

Bob's resume to the right hiring manager at Chevron. Bob got an interview. Interestingly, Bob had applied online for many Chevron jobs but never got a response. The college connection and request for help got him in front of someone in power and it opened the door. Bob did the rest. He excelled when given his chance, and Bob landed his dream job at Chevron.

College networks are truly gold mines. Several of my clients have reported it opened the door and gave them the extra help they needed to land the job.

CHAPTER 9
WHAT YOU NEED TO KNOW
ABOUT RECRUITERS

"Good things come to those who hustle
while they wait."

ROBIN RYAN

There are two different types of recruiters out there now. You may be familiar with executive recruiters; perhaps one helped you to land a previous job. Their numbers are shrinking as companies move away from this expensive recruiting option.

On the rise, and very popular in high-tech and large companies, are internal HR recruiters employed by a company to seek out and find top talent, then connect those candidates with internal decision makers for jobs that company has available.

INTERNAL HR RECRUITERS

These internal employees spend their days looking for talent. They are on websites, at blogs, and in chat rooms, but mostly they

150

network like you wouldn't believe to dig up talented candidates. They place ads on the job boards or their own company's website. They are *very* influential and have power over whether or not you get hired. Do not confuse the recruiters with a typical HR person who screens applicants or sorts resumes, attends to administrative tasks for current employees, and has little to no say in the hiring process. HR recruiters have a great deal of influence with the hiring manager.

Internal recruiters can take you out of the running. They usually know a lot about their jobs and the business units they serve. They will screen you by phone to identify your true skill set. If you come across as a high-potential employee, they will connect you to the decision maker. Whenever possible, don't overlook the technique of getting an inside friend to send the internal recruiter your resume. This can open the door for you. Internal referrals are an important aspect of the hiring process. These recruiters fill internal jobs because they are *cost-effective* for the employer. More and more companies have stopped using outside agencies; they have hired permanent employees to conduct their recruiting tasks from people who gained their experience in search firms. The number of internal HR recruiters continues to grow, so be on the lookout for these internal people who can help you land the job you want.

EXECUTIVE RECRUITERS

These recruiters work for the employers who have hired them, not for you. They do not work to help you find a job. They work to help their client — the employer — to successfully fill a position. They are not career counselors, and they only "place" people who fit the search profile they are currently pursuing. In fact most executive recruiters place fewer than twenty candidates a *year!* For top executives, they may handle only five or six placements in a twelve-month period.

Typically these types of recruiters are working in either one of two ways:

1. Retained search
2. Contingency basis

In a *retained search,* the recruiter is paid by clients to fill specific positions. Never be confused that this recruiter cares about you or your career. She has a specific profile she is looking for; you may have excellent experience, but if you lack the MBA she requires, for example, she'll tell you no, and this employer won't hire you. Try not to take it personally. She talks to many people but must dig up the exact skill set the employer wants or lose the paying customer.

Typically in a retained search the recruiter first tries to find people from a target list of the company's competitors. She puts together a "short list" of prospective candidates for her client. Prior to that, she has determined which of those candidates on the short list have the exact industry or market knowledge, leadership skills, and record of performance the employer wants. She has also predetermined that these candidates are interested in the job, fall in the salary range the employer is willing to pay, and will relocate if that is necessary. Once they've been heavily screened and prepped by the recruiter, the candidates meet with the company's decision-making team.

Retained searches are at play in various industries.

These days, you may see them used to find executives at high levels, e.g., CEOs or nonprofit leaders, top local or county government administrators, and college deans, school superintendents, etc.

In *contingency-based searches,* the recruiter only gets paid *if* he is successful in placing a candidate. He serves as the middleman to bring the two parties together. He may present just one candidate, or he may present several to the prospective employer. It's important to note that in these kinds of searches, the employer is likely using various tools besides this recruiter to find you, such as other recruiters, its own HR department, referrals, and job boards. So if the candidate the contingency-based recruiter is putting forward loses out to another candidate, then this recruiter does not get paid. Therefore his objective is to *get his candidate hired.*

A basic difference between retainer and contingency recruiters, then, is that *a retained search always represents the client (the employer); the contingency-based search often represents the candidate but only insomuch as that candidate has the exact skills the employer wants.* An exception exists. That is where a contingency recruiter secures an exclusive (but still contingency) contract to fill a position — meaning that particular recruiter is the only recruiter working on the position. In this situation the recruiter may act like a retained recruiter — presenting the position as his or hers and offering several candidates to the client —

even if the client also may be generating candidates on its own. Only if one of these recruiter's candidates is selected will he or she get paid.

Executive recruiters typically specialize. They handle one field, such as accounting or finance, health care, or sales across various industries. Others may work a sector, recruiting various jobs within, say, the academic arena. For a comprehensive list of the ten thousand–plus executive recruiters working in the United States, see the bible of recruiters: *The Directory of Executive and Professional Recruiters* put out by Kennedy Information (WWW.KENNEDYINFO.COM).

TIP: Executive search firms fill a minuscule percentage of the openings available at any given time. Do not spend much time trying to develop this source unless they have an opening you are definitely and completely qualified to perform, such as an MD, general counsel, city manager, CEO, school superintendent, etc.

■ ■ ■ ■

PART 3
RESUMES AND COVER LETTERS

■ ■ ■ ■

"A dream is just a dream, but a goal is a dream with a plan and a deadline."

ROBIN RYAN

CHAPTER 10
YOUR TARGETED RESUME

"When the competition is keen,
remember, there is only one you."
ROBIN RYAN

Only fifteen seconds! That's all you get when a decision maker, human resource manager, or staff person sorts out resumes. Just a fifteen-second glance! So it better be good or they'll all pass you by.

Being over 40 does have a significant effect on your resume. Boston College published a study on hiring practices, featuring a person applying to jobs in Boston and St. Petersburg, Florida. Posing as a female job applicant, researchers sent out four thousand resumes. The resumes varied the year of high school graduation, which dated the job seeker as being anywhere from ages 35 to 62. The results determined that younger women were *40% more likely* to receive an offer for a job interview than women over

50. The answer to this issue is: have a terrific resume, noting only relevant material that supports the job you are going after. You may also find it helpful to limit your work history and remove the graduation year from college degrees.

Many resumes of people over 40 are downright terrible. Their resume *is* a major stumbling block to their getting hired. This advertisement must be the very best representative of yourself possible, with only one purpose in mind — to get an interview.

SELL YOUR ASSETS

Focus on results! DMs want to know all about your accomplishments. Resumes that get interviews clearly demonstrate this one important message: actions equal results.

Use descriptive action verbs to describe your experience and include the positive results that your actions achieved. That's *positive* — they don't have to be *stellar*. Don't discount your achievements because you feel what you did is not a big deal. A client once told me she had no accomplishments. Nothing she'd done had produced big results. She was a great paperwork organizer. "Paper flow is no big deal," she'd tell me. Yet it saved employees time and the company money, and it improved customer service by introducing a more efficient process. That's what she had to sell.

Results sell! So sell your results!

At 40 you have acquired a nice track record with some accomplishments that *can* help you beat out the competition. At 45 you are competing against those eager-beaver people in their 30s, but, again, you can illustrate your initiative and show how you have solved problems and delivered results. By 50 you are competing with a lot of accomplished folks. So focus on selling your best skills and accomplishments to get the results done for the position you are applying for. *Your resume needs to really promote the results you have achieved in the more recent past positions.* Note anything new you have learned lately to make you more valuable to the employer. Show where you implemented positive change. Explain where you made productivity and process improvements. Emphasize where you made money, saved money, saved time, or contained costs. I have seen horrific resumes from professionals and executives who are over 40. I could write dozens of pages on resume mistakes. Many people just dust off an old one and do not take the hours necessary to create a good resume that effectively advertises their accomplishments. Employers focus on progressive success — and delivery of results. They look at your potential to perform their job well. You have only seconds to capture their interest as they look at your resume. It must be impressive. However much time it takes, yours needs to be top-notch.

MUST-USE RESUME SECRETS EMPLOYERS LOVE

When I did a national survey of six hundred hiring managers, the overwhelming majority said the most important part of your resume is your "Summary of Qualifications" section. This is a high-impact section. Employers reported that this was one of the very first areas they read. And if the briefly stated summary demonstrates a solid ability to fill the advertised job, it catches their attention and they slow down and give the applicant more careful consideration.

Hiring managers also reported that only about 5% of resumes sent out by those over 40 contain this key section. I never write a resume without it. Think of it as a highly influential summation of the specifics you bring to the job. This section usually consists of four to six sentences that present an overview of your experience, accomplishments, talents, work habits, and skills. Here is one client's example — she got several interviews and landed a good position with a significant salary increase.

Summary Of Qualifications

Proven leadership directing the Human Resources divisions for billion-dollar organization. Delivered notable cost-saving results, operational improvements, and productivity increases. Demonstrated organizational development expertise, responding to changing business objectives and needs in fast-changing environment. Core competencies include: strategic planning, project management, communications, employee development, and implementation skills. Expert level in HR information systems managing the implementation of employee education on the Intranet/Internet using Web-based tools. Recognized for developing award-winning team members that achieve business and customer results.

The "summary of qualifications" section, which speaks volumes by consolidating the best you have to bring to the job, really stands out and pulls the employer in for a closer look. Be sure that your resume has this essential section.

ACCEPTABLE RESUME FORMAT STYLES

Only two styles of resume formats are widely accepted for those over 40: *chronological* and *combination*. Employers dislike a third style, called the "functional" resume, and I no longer use this style for anyone. The functional resume highlights major areas of accomplishments and skills, but does not show employers where you did any of it. In fact, work history is at the bottom of the resume and deemphasized. Resume writers use this style to *hide* things — and employers know it. You can cover up job-hopping, hide work gaps and lack of history, bury nonreflective titles — anything you feel is weak. Some people may not have had much paid experience but do have a lot of ability that they've acquired through volunteering or working with civic groups and the like, so resume creators may use this format to draw attention to their abilities and skills — focusing on what they can do, not where they did it. It is most commonly used for changing careers, reentering the workforce, and finding entry-level positions. I strongly suggest you do not use it.

Hiring managers and HR professionals are big critics of this style.

The two resume formatting styles you can choose from are these:

- **CHRONOLOGICAL RESUME** (see samples for Sam and Daniel in chapter 12). The chronological resume is organized by employment dates, beginning with your most recent job, followed by the one before that, and so on. It emphasizes the job title, the experience acquired there, and the employer you worked for. This resume style demonstrates a progressive career path and is usually very easy to follow. It's commonly used when career direction is very clear, you have had significant promotions, and your job target is directly in line with your previous work history. Executive recruiters love this style, as they want to document *all* of your experience. You see it quite often in the fields of science, finance, medicine, engineering, academia, and senior management. Don't use the chronological resume if you've got a spotty work history, if you're a career changer, or if you have changed jobs frequently. Use this style to emphasize your job titles and the employers you worked for. Chronological works best for those over 40 who have had good employers and good job titles, and who can demonstrate from their experience at prestigious institutions or companies how they would come into a new organization now and do a very effective job.

- **COMBINATION RESUME** (see samples for Alena, Steve, John, and Mary in chapter 12). A combination resume will list your job titles and employers, and it will explain your experience using subheadings, breaking them into two or three skill areas. This style allows you to not repeat yourself and really focus on stressing your accomplishments. I like this highly acceptable format a great deal. It can have amazing impact. HR managers and decision makers find it easier to read and grasp what you can do for them. This format allows you to advertise your qualifications by using functional sections, plus it emphasizes where you got the experience. This format works well, particularly for people who have worked many years with one employer. It's easy to read and quickly showcases the complex abilities you bring to a position.

Keeping your resume relevant to the job you are applying for, being concise, and covering the last five to seven years in detail is the best way to impress employers. To control page length, go back twelve to fifteen years maximum. If your goal is not to reveal your age, limit the work history to no more than fifteen years, and in the section on your education do not mention when you earned your degrees. This is rarely necessary but sometimes it does help not to announce your age. If you seek a senior-level position, though, keep in mind that almost no one reaches these jobs by age 30. In fact, employers expect — *and want* — their executives to have a lot of experience before they run their big programs, divisions, departments, or companies. In these cases, do not remove the graduation years . . . they will not hurt you in the least, as your experience is one of your better assets for succeeding in the job.

CHAPTER 11
GUIDELINES ON FORMATTING
AND WRITING YOUR RESUME

"Believe in yourself,
and you will be unstoppable."

ROBIN RYAN

Formatting is essential to make your resume look good. Your objective is to get the attention of the reader long enough to make a positive impression. Use white space, italics, capital letters, underlining, boldface, indentations, and bullets to emphasize your important points. No graphics, no colored fonts, no lines across the page. No fonts smaller than 11 point, 12 being the right size for most of your text. Arial and Helvetica are good clean fonts that are easy to read. Don't use abbreviations or acronyms. Though both may be very familiar to you, someone screening your resume for the hiring boss may not recognize those things and screen you out because he didn't see the skills the boss told him to look for.

FORMATTING AND LAYOUT GUIDELINES

Make your resume look professional and attractive so it is easy to read. Here are some layout and structural guidelines:

SOFTWARE: Use MS Word

MARGINS: 0.7 inches — top, bottom, and sides

FONT SIZE: 12 point — your name in 14 point

FONT: Easy to read — Arial is a good choice

NAME AND ADDRESS: Centered on top of page. Name: bolded and in a slightly larger font size (14 point) than address (12 point). Phone: clear and easy-to-read numbers — use home number and/or cell, not work number. Email: clear and easy to read — home only, not work. Be professional; make sure your name appears as part of this email address.

Kathleen Smith, MBA
1 Main Street
City, WA 98111
(425) 555-1112
name@msn.com

HEADINGS: Centered, bolded, small

caps; in this order:

CAREER OBJECTIVE
SUMMARY OF QUALIFICATIONS
PROFESSIONAL EXPERIENCE
EDUCATION
AWARDS AND HONORS — OPTIONAL
COMPUTER SKILLS — OPTIONAL
RELOCATION — OPTIONAL
FOREIGN LANGUAGE — OPTIONAL
TECHNICAL SKILLS — OPTIONAL

EXAMPLE:
CAREER OBJECTIVE: DIRECTOR OF STRATEGIC PLANNING

PROFESSIONAL EXPERIENCE: Job title in italics, then company/city/state/dates of employment in regular text.

EXAMPLE:
VP Finance, Big Company, Boston, MA, 2008–present

JOB FUNCTION: Use subheads, bolded — underlined optional.

EXAMPLE:
International Business

BULLETS/DASHES: Align all bullets under heading, as follows.

EXAMPLE:

Leadership
- Led a national nonprofit organization for eight years, consisting of 32 employees, 24,000 members, and a $16.5 million annual budget.

EDUCATION: Degrees first, then licenses, certifications held.

EDUCATION

MBA, Simmons College, Boston, MA, 1994

BS, Accounting/Business Management, University of Massachusetts, Boston, MA

CPA — Massachusetts — inactive

WRITING SECRETS TO USE

These strategies will help you to avoid key mistakes and to develop a resume that grabs decision makers' attention.

Tailor Your Resume Specifically to the Job

You have so many skills, so many things that you could do. Many over-40 candidates include virtually everything they have ever done. Everything! A resume like this reads like one very long job description, or worse, an autobiography. Employers say that broad, general resumes are a worthless effort. The employer will not take the time to look through an unfocused resume to determine a person's skills. If you don't clearly illustrate the job you seek, and illuminate your skills and your accomplishments so they jump off the paper, you are sunk. Edit and edit again. Focus on relevance to the job title you seek and eliminate any words and phrases that don't support how you perform at that level and title.

Limit Length to Two Pages

HR people make snap judgments. Oftentimes, less carries more impact. A two-page resume is the maximum length for *anyone* over 40. An HR representative at a Fortune 100 company who has reviewed thousands of resumes said that a major mistake, from her perspective, is candidates offering too much information, 50% of which is useless. I agree (having seen people submit eight to ten pages and calling it a resume). *Results and accomplishments,* not lengthy job duties and descriptions, are what gets an employer's attention. Focusing on the last five to seven years of experience will help eliminate extra pages.

Add Keywords

Keywords are critical in an online review —
without the right ones your resume never
pops out of cyberspace. The solution is to
find the magical words that will virtually
guarantee that employers discover your
resume and call you in for an interview. But
the catch is that *there's a different set of
magic words for every employer and for every
job.* The person conducting the search picks
some arbitrary words to use to sort out the
resumes. You have no way of knowing what
those keywords are. This is a problem.
Today, with more employers accepting
electronic resumes, they rely more on
keywords to sift through them all to find
the "right" job candidates they want to
interview. It is an amazingly complex system
and very difficult for you to get noticed in.
Often a company receives thousands of
electronically submitted resumes. (Many
Fortune 500 companies report getting more
than 100,000 resumes *every month.*) Typically, larger companies and governmental
agencies (usually with more than 2,000
employees) run some type of employment
recruiting software, with a keyword-
searchable database, to isolate the resumes

that fit their job vacancies. Your best option is to make an educated guess as to the skills and qualifications you need to incorporate as keywords on your resume.

Keywords are industry, or job-specific, terms. So, how can you figure out what those magic words are? Most keywords are nouns. Job seekers have long been taught to emphasize action verbs in their job search correspondence, and that advice is still valid. Keywords may include a specific skill like staff training or Java programming, or a certain college degree like a bachelor's or master's. The employer continues to narrow the search, looking for other important skills or experience; for example, they'd search the underlined words:

- Handled <u>cross-functional communications</u>.
- Coordinated <u>marketing campaigns</u> and <u>special events</u>.
- Managed numerous <u>process improvements</u>.
- <u>MBA</u>.

Notice these are specifically related to the experience the employer is looking for in a candidate. Keywords they almost always seek out are the precise job title, essential certifications, specific tasks or duties, even zip codes, for narrowing down searches geographically.

The best method to use to uncover good keywords is to scrutinize employment ads placed by employers. Review the major things they ask for. Check several ads and you should get a feel for what keywords are repeatedly mentioned in association with a given job title. Incorporate those keywords throughout the resume.

I try to front-load the resume with keywords in the first bullet description I write. This works well too. Most applicant-search software not only looks for keywords but also ranks them on a weighted basis according to the importance of the word to the job criteria. Some keywords are considered mandatory, and others are merely desirable. Your resume can also be ranked according to how many times mandatory words appear in your resume. If your document contains no mandatory keywords, the keyword search obviously will overlook your resume. Those with the greatest "keyword density" will be chosen for the next round of screening, this time by a human. Generally, the more specific a keyword is to a particular job or industry, the more heavily it will be weighted. Skills that apply to many jobs and industries tend to be weighted less heavily.

Don't Exaggerate or Lie

Employers are well aware that many people lie on their resume. Recent executive surveys revealed that 33% of people who claimed they had completed degrees hadn't earned them, and more than 52% of executives had exaggerated their job titles and accomplishments.

Solid facts and verifiable experience should highlight your *actions* and *accomplishments.*

Entrepreneur Donald Trump, who owns and manages hotels and casinos and hosts TV shows, summed it up nicely, saying: "It used to be that if you wanted to get a better job, you didn't think twice about padding your resume just a little bit. Maybe you lied about a degree here and there or about playing on your college football team. But employers are getting wise — and worried — about those kinds of deceptions and have increasingly hired special companies to do background checks on candidates before they ever get a job offer. What's the harm, you wonder, in a few minor deceptions? Those lies can come back to haunt you. Recently, resume inaccuracies have ruined the careers of executives at several organizations. This is serious stuff. Good executives don't want liars to lead their companies. And you can't blame them. After all, if you don't think twice about lying on a job application, chances are you cheat in your day-to-day business dealings. Here's my advice. Don't lie. Figure out a way to tell the truth and still make yourself look good."

Clarify Your Job Focus
If the purpose of a resume is to get an interview, then you must know what kind of job you're looking for. You can have more than one resume. Many over-40 professionals have a lot of work experience and could do more than one specific job. Your career objective is the job title you're looking for — for each career objective, write a different resume. For example, suppose you want a job as a fund-raiser or executive director of a nonprofit agency. You need two resumes: the fund-raiser one will focus on all the fund-raising and event-planning work you've done. Your second resume, for executive director of a nonprofit, would mention fund-raising in a minor way but play up administrative skills, hiring, budgeting, management, etc. Same person, same background, but each resume uses your back-

ground to highlight the most relevant accomplishments *to support the stated career objective.* State a clear and simple career objective (your target job) to prevent your resume from being undirected. Use a job title — e.g., "trainer." Lengthy career objectives no longer work and are very ineffective. A concise resume that focuses on your abilities to do the job for which you are applying will get you more interviews.

Use Action Verbs and Descriptive Terms

Action verbs will help you improve your work description and better illustrate your accomplishments. Action verbs can make a difference. Select words that clearly and succinctly describe the kind of action you've done. Never use the word "I" in your resume.

Quantify to Add Impact

Throughout your resume, think action and results. There are easy ways to do this. Think about things in terms of what you "increased" or "decreased." Use percentages, such as "Implemented new customer service program, which increased our retention of clients by 20%." You can estimate these figures. Don't exaggerate, but give a clear and accurate estimate. Statistics add a lot of power to a resume. Use numbers wherever they make sense, for example, "Supervised two people" might not be as effective as saying "Supervisory skills." But if you supervised 50 people, then you might say "Supervised a department with 50 employees." This shows the actions and the resulting accomplishment. Include statistics, percentages, increases, decreases, cost savings, anything that really quantifies your skills.

Proofread! Again!

Proofread to correct spelling, grammar, syntax, and punctuation. In other words, be perfect! It's a good idea to have someone else proof your resume to catch any mistakes you might have missed. A good resume must be a perfect advertisement. Just one mistake can mean no interviews.

Analyze Accomplishments

Most of us find it difficult to brag about ourselves. Yet when you create a resume that doesn't clearly show the accomplishments and results your actions have achieved, you almost always fail. Why? Employers want to hire candidates who they believe will come in and deliver the needed performance to get their job done, and done well. For example, one client listed his accomplishments by creating one highly notable point that summarized the major actions and the results he achieved:

- Spent four years as a store manager and made significant improvements in team performance, store appearance, and enhanced customer loyalty that improved repeat business. *Results increased the store sales by 31%.*

Analyze your past jobs and write out the duties. Next, highlight your achievements and then select those that should be incorporated into your resume based on relevance to the job you seek. Strong descriptive actions that concisely show the key tangible result is the goal. Employers judge an applicant they know only on paper by the written actions and achievements that resulted from your efforts. Make sure you include any actions that involved creating something new, being innovative, or developing process improvements, as these constitute the "results" employers search for. Be sure to edit and keep your resume clear, concise, and succinct so your accomplishments will stand out.

Make it the Best You Can

I repeatedly hear from job hunters that resume writing is not easy when you need to create one for yourself. Agreed. It's not easy, but it is a very essential piece to your job search success and so you need to invest the time and energy to make yours be top-notch.

Most people find it takes *many* hours to produce a good resume. The process takes time, both for the necessary inner analysis and thought and for the writing of duties, noting of accomplishments, and editing. Then you must make sure the information is presented in a concise but easy to glean way.

You don't have to do it alone, though. You should consider getting feedback from someone who hires a lot of people, or who works in HR and handles recruiting and screening. But keep in mind, many HR folks don't manage the resume sorting and selection process, so not just anyone in an HR department can give you solid direction or advice. There are professionals who can help you too, plus numerous books with formulas and strategies to follow.

The bottom line is this: poor resumes will get no interviews. A good resume can yield ten times more interviews than an average one. Make yours great!

CHAPTER 12
RESUME SAMPLES

"He who dares — wins!"

ROBIN RYAN

One picture — or in this case, one resume sample — can be worth a thousands words.

Below are some actual client resumes that I created, which landed each client interviews and helped him or her get a new job. Minor changes were made to protect their privacy, such as their names and addresses, but otherwise these are the exact resumes they submitted.

RESUME: SENIOR EXECUTIVE — LAID OFF

Sam, age 47, was highly accomplished but had moved a great deal for his jobs and promotions. His wife refused to move again, which meant a big problem for his career and job search. His former company had given him a severance package. Highly paid jobs are difficult to find and there were few to none in his industry where he lived. That meant changing fields — not easy to do when you earn over $225,000 in base salary annually, with big bonus opportunities and stock options. His original resume had several problems: the format was very poorly done, making it hard to read; the graphic lines were a big no-no; he used too many abbreviations; and the small font size made it hard to glean anything from the resume with a quick glance. Sam had an MBA, but that degree was buried at the end of his multi-page resume. It was not after his name and many people likely missed it when reviewing his resume. Sam and I spent several hours creating the resume below. It was highly effective and got him several interviews. He successfully changed fields and went to work for a high-tech company. Networking, along with his new resume, opened the door for him.

Sam Harrington, MBA

1 Main Street • City, USA 11111
123.555.1212 cell • name@verizon.net

CAREER OBJECTIVE: VP SALES/NEW BUSINESS DEVELOPMENT

SUMMARY OF QUALIFICATIONS

Results-driven senior executive with an award-winning proven track record in leadership, sales, and new business development for a multi-billion-dollar company, having delivered hundreds of millions of dollars in increased revenues. P&L responsibility with expertise in consumer product sales, licensing, and partnership building to expand sales opportunities and revenues worldwide. Described as the "get it done guy" who excels in development and implementation of strategy and tactics to launch, expand, and grow new or existing businesses. Recognized for building highly productive teams that continuously exceed goals and expectations, plus rated as one of the top managers company-wide.

PROFESSIONAL EXPERIENCE

Kraft Foods, Northfield, Illinois, 2002–present

Vice President Sales, Global Consumer Products Sales, *2004–present*

- Established a new sales strategy to relaunch an unprofitable product line. Developed new partners and distribution deals with Costco, Sam's, Wal-Mart, Target, Office Max, Office Depot, Walgreens, and others. Set up new operations and processes. Contracted with new vendors and distributors. *Results generated $22M in new revenues and licensing fees.*

- Analyzed the business position and pricing for U.S. markets. Developed new joint-venture sales strategy and built consensus among all joint-venture partners. *Results raised pricing 13.4%, earning over $65M in additional revenue.*

- Developed a new strategy to reduce U.S. channel advertising dollars by 20%. Implemented new tactics to elevate product positioning, retain brand premium appeal, and continue to drive sales. *Results maintained sales levels and saved company $15M.*

- Established the business strategy for global product sales involving brand positioning, sales tactics, channels, package, marketing, and distribution in Asia, Europe, Canada, and Mexico. Worked collaboratively enterprise-wide to extend or create new global partnerships. Launched new products in Europe and Asia. *Results added $200M in new revenues.*

promoted from *Vice President of Sales,* Nabisco, 2005–2008

- Led the repositioning of product line after acquired by Nabisco. Established new sales strategy and marketing campaign that improved brand awareness. Added special promotional events. Developed new specialized in-store merchandizing marketing displays that enhanced sales. Completely revamped advertising tactics and tools. Hired new sales teams. *Results increased sales from $8.7M to $27M, a 309% increase over three years.*

- Managed the comprehensive sales business unit, having P&L responsibility with a $74M budget. Handled all domestic and international sales planning/merchandizing; customer service; and inside sales. Oversaw 27 direct reports, outside field reps, and multiple distribution systems.

- Hired new executives that improved programs involving accountability and auditing over field performance that improved execution and effectiveness of advertising spending. *Results made product the fastest growing in niche channels, with 30% sales growth in a 52-week period.*

promoted from *Grocery Sales Director,* Kraft, 2004–2005

- Developed the new business strategy and comprehensive business plan to expand sales by adding new products. Created forecasts; projected expenditures and P&Ls. Built consensus throughout numerous business units enterprise-wide to green-light project. Established initial sales program, pitching sales to C-level and senior executives of potential partners, selling to Safeway, Albertson's, Kroger, and Target. *Results generated over $200M revenues from inception.*

- Hired and trained the sales team on the grocery strategy, goals, and objectives. Developed and led the "train-the-trainer" program for in-store employees involving national accounts including: Albertson's Corporate, Safeway Corporate, Target, Kroger Divisions, etc.

promoted from *Grocery Marketing Director,* Kraft, 2003–2004

- Developed the business plan and sold the concept departmentally to Kraft Senior Management team. Developed grocery strategy, goals, target customers, objectives, and selling materials. Revamped development team and the process for developing grocery locations, reducing cost and time from the process. *Results saved 10% in overall costs.*

promoted from *Grocery Sales Manager,* Kraft, 2002–2003

- Launched new product into the grocery channel and developed a Trade Marketing Management System and forecasting tools.

Midwest Regional Manager, Gatorade, Portland, Oregon, 2000–2002

- Directed broker sales organizations in the Northwest with 15% of the divisional business. Developed a sales plan that *resulted in achieving 68% of the division's sales.*

Borden, Inc., Columbus, Ohio, 1992–1999

Director — Sales Planning; promoted from **Regional Manager — Sauce and Seafood Division;** promoted from **Manager — Sales Planning**

- Directed and trained Sales Planning Managers, setting goals and objectives. Created numerous new computerized business systems including: Sales Budgeting, Sales Incentive, Broker Incentive, Performance Planning, Brand Promotional, and Accrual Spending Tracking. *Results allowed for improved auditing and cost containment.*

Procter & Gamble, Various Locations, 1987–1991

Special Assignment — Sales Technology; promoted from *Unit Manager — Health & Personal Care;* promoted from *District Field Representative;* promoted from *Sales Manager*

• Promoted three times in five years. Developed new prototype system adopted throughout P&G. *Results improved merchandizing performance, contributing significantly to bottom-line sales.*

AWARDS AND HONORS

President's Award, Exceptional
Performance, Kraft, four given
enterprise-wide, 2006
Top Regional Sales Manager,
companywide, Borden, 1996
Top Performing Division, retail areas,
Procter & Gamble, 1989

EDUCATION

MBA, Marketing Finance, Suffolk
University, Boston, MA, 1996
BS, Organizational Communications,
University of Connecticut, Storrs, 1986

RESUME: FORTUNE 500 MANAGER — RETIRED AT 53, RETURNING TO WORK AT 56

Alena, in her mid-50s, had actually left the work world behind until the stock market wiped out a great deal of her savings. That event forced her to job hunt. Originally from India, she had been out of the workplace over four years. Her original resume was full of everything she'd ever done, in detail. It was five pages long — with too much dated information that no employer would care about. She had too many things going on — extensively describing each tech job she'd ever held and listing software programs that were outdated and no longer used. The font size was too small and the complex format compounded the readability problems. Alena also had listed all her degrees, including a recent degree in philosophy. This took the focus away from her math and computer science degrees, so we decided to leave it off the resume. The new resume we created made a major difference. It was highly effective and landed her a new job in a matter of weeks.

Alena Gupta
1 Main Street
City, USA 11111
123.555.1212 cell
name@verizon.net

CAREER OBJECTIVE: PROGRAM MANAGER — IT AND CLIENT SERVICES

SUMMARY OF QUALIFICATIONS

Proven track record leading Fortune 100 company teams working on cutting-edge technologies and customer applications for large clients. Responsible for client relations and providing world-class customer service, and pre- and post-technical sales support. Displayed entrepreneurial drive directing the analysis, design, and application development using creative problem solving to deliver new innovations and business solutions. Developed numerous employee training programs on emerging technologies that advanced employee skills and operational abilities. Strengths include: building productive teams, client relations, technical troubleshooting, inventing new solutions, training and curriculum development, communications, and interpersonal skills.

PROFESSIONAL EXPERIENCE

President, Benton Consulting Inc., Oakland, CA, 2004–2007

Senior Software Consultant, Digital Equipment Corporation, Boston, MA, 1982–2003

Other positions: Software Business Unit Manager, AI Architect, Senior Educational Specialist

Business Unit Management

• Managed the software services business unit for a Fortune 100 company, overseeing staff of thirty. Responsibilities included: client relations; technical sales support; client requirements/ needs analysis; hired/developed/ coached staff; budget management; logistics; deliverables; scheduling; process development/implementation; coordination of multifunctional teams; cross-divisional communication; resources allocations; quality assurance; meeting milestones/deadlines on time.

- Developed the new data center business unit focused on technical applications for large technical customers (Lockheed, GE, Schlumberger). Hired team. Implemented new business strategy. Added new products and services. *Results grew this business unit 900% over a two-year period.*

- Established processes, procedures, and systems for supporting large and small customers involving presales/postsales support, upgrades, and maintenance.

- Worked with senior management to establish global plan, milestones, goals, and tactical plans.

- Planned, executed, and successfully managed concurrent technology projects for various customers. Handled internal and external communications, workflow, and change management.

Applications Consulting — Analysis and Design

- Led numerous projects creating leading-edge technology and utilizing it to develop workable business solutions that resulted in improved operations, better support for customers. *Results added significant revenue increases to company's bottom line.*

- Evaluated numerous emerging technologies. Analyzed potential and business applications of these technologies. Conducted feasibility studies. Developed customized customer products. Created customer training programs usage and operations.

- Designed new models with coding to implement applications using the workflow methodology.

- Conducted comprehensive analysis of customer business needs and technical problems. Developed prototypes to demonstrate usage functions. Generated models and new designs to deliver workable business solutions.

- Performed programming, tuning, code profiling, code review, architecture, plus analysis and design in support of key business initiatives.

- Managed complex IT projects, working seamlessly between cross-functional teams.

- Supervised teams of up to thirty people, including managing virtual teams and outsourced teams.

Training

- Developed employee training programs for engineering and programming groups.

- Conducted extensive analysis of job duties, expectations, and performance levels to identify training needs. Created original and innovative employee training programs by developing curriculum to teach needed skills and how-to operations on new technologies.

Technology Skills

Languages: C, C++, Java, SQL, C#, Visual Basic, XML, html

Operating systems: Windows, Windows NT

Platforms: Microsoft, Forte

Specialty applications: OO methodologies and tools; AI methodologies and tools; client server applications

EDUCATION

BS, Mathematics and Computer Science — Florida State University, Tallahassee, 1981

BS, Statistics, Mathematics and Physics — Osmania University, Hyderabad, India

HONORS AND AWARDS

Outstanding Performance Awards in Software Services, Digital Equipment Corporation

RESUME: SENIOR EXECUTIVE — EMPLOYED

Steve, in his early 50s, came to see me because he despised his new boss. The health-care organization had gone through a merger and he found himself losing a job he loved, facing potential demotion, and having to work for a year for a man who did not want him as his legal counsel. He lived in a small city and knew that relocation would be essential for a new job. Still, with a very demanding fulltime job, he had only a few hours to devote to job hunting. The old resume had failed miserably to secure him interviews. It was too long to begin with. When a recruiter told him five pages was too much, he shrank the font size to 10 point, thus cramming it into three pages — eliminating nothing. Other problems included poor formatting, too much capitalization, heavy use of graphic lines, and too many bullets. The senior executive summary was confusing; it lacked results statements; and it used very lengthy job descriptions. His resume needed to be clearer to recruiters, and it had to promote the results he had achieved. His new resume got him an interview everywhere he applied. He accepted a new position in California, one that came with a major signing bonus, a $55,000 salary increase, and a very attractive relocation package with significant house-buying/selling coverage.

Steven Huscroft, JD

1 Main Street
City, USA 11111
123.555.1212 cell
name@verizon.net

CAREER OBJECTIVE: LEGAL COUNSEL POSITION

SUMMARY OF QUALIFICATIONS

Ten years experience as in-house general counsel, recognized for outstanding employee performance directing the legal department and corporate governance for billion-dollar healthcare organizations. Responsible for: establishing legal strategy, vision, direction, team development, board/executives' advisement, plus management of legal disputes dealing with complex liability, fraud, abuse, and employment issues. A results-driven global thinker who helped to design and implement an enterprise-wide quality improvement initiative that delivered measurable outcomes. Creative problem solver who excels at: strategy, change management, negotiations, mediation, regulatory compliance, and establishment of policies and systems that reduce liability and risk.

PROFESSIONAL EXPERIENCE

Regional Vice President/General Counsel, Centura Health, Englewood, CO, 2003–present

Regional Vice President, Catholic Health Initiatives, Kansas City, MO, 1999–2003

Associate General Counsel, Iowa Health System, Des Moines, IA, 1989–1999

Leadership

- Served as general counsel for ten years for two major healthcare systems *($5B in revenues, up to 70 hospitals and 40 long-term care facilities)* providing legal direction, strategy, counsel/advice, and crisis management. Duties included: mergers; acquisitions; regulatory compliance; physician relations; strategic planning; negotiations; mediation; labor/employment law; litigation management; hiring outside counsel; project management; governmental operations; executive/board advisement, plus consultant to internal department heads; JCAHO ethics compliance; and HIPAA management.

- Created new legal departments for all three employers. Established all policies, procedures, processes, systems, and best practices for the delivery of legal services across multistate locations. Hired, trained, supervised, and mentored team of six.

- Served as a major executive contributor on the long-term strategic program to make Centura's organization an "employer of choice" by improving employee relations and retention. Led the team to develop and distribute employee satisfaction survey. Conducted interviews of department heads, staff, and medical teams for input to improve workplace experience for employees. Responsible for planning, development, and implementation of the improved workplace initiative over a two-year period. *Results improved employee satisfaction from 60% to 69%, and reduced attrition.*

- Led the acquisition team working as liaison to outside counsel overseeing the 2008 acquisition process taking over and assimilating a $230M hospital and several physician clinics. Conducted all due diligence and negotiations, and managed the contractual transaction.

• Reorganized the legal department and the organization's delivery of legal services. Cross-trained existing staff to reduce outside legal fees, established in-house workers compensation program, and improved labor/employment practices. *Results saved $600,000 in first year of implementation.*

Legal Strategy/Litigation Management

• Managed the legal process handling a very large-scale complex lawsuit brought against the organization involving Medicare fraud and abuse that threatened the survivability of a hospital. Hired, managed, and directed outside litigators while overseeing ongoing processing of this lawsuit.

• Directed the legal process involving crisis situations and partnership with police and FBI handling high-profile cases involving hospital staff, kidnapping, and parental refusal of medical treatment.

• Managed several legal situations involving liability issues, human resources/EEOC/disgruntled employee/wrongful dismissal complaints, discrimination accusations, and breach of contracts. Resolved suits satisfactorily in organization's favor.

• Developed and implemented new hospital and long-term care facilities' processes, procedures, and systems to reduce liability and risk plus successfully reduce drug diversion.

• Led the legal strategy, oversaw litigation management, plus conducted damage control involving lawsuit filed on constitutional law issues and medical rights in an ongoing legal case with extensive media scrutiny and national healthcare ramifications.

• Provided legal counsel and advised Board of Directors and Executive Team on operational, governance, corporate bylaw, human resources, li-

ability, and business issues, plus oversaw organization's trademark and
copyright protections.

Contract Negotiations and Mediation

• Managed organization's response to a
media-driven lawsuit filed by doctors
for breach of contract. Served as piv-
otal liaison to all parties including the
media, internal physicians, executive
team, and Board of Directors. Settled
case without payment. Mediated issues
to amicably resolve suit.

• Led hundreds of contract negotiations
involving physician and group agreements, business transactions, leases,
employee termination agreements,
subcontractors, vendors, property
acquisitions, plus managed care/
insurance agreements.

• Negotiated and implemented a physician quality improvement program for
specialty programs.

Regulatory Compliance

- Designed an enterprise-wide regulatory compliance program for Catholic Health Initiatives and led the implementation of the new program throughout eight hospitals and eight long-term care facilities in four states.

- Served as liaison to governmental agencies and regulatory officers regarding any fraud and abuse.

- Led the multidisciplinary team to develop and implement HIPAA/ privacy policies throughout hospitals and physician clinics to meet all governmental regulatory requirements.

- Worked cooperatively with federal agencies handling internal employment/personnel audits.

EDUCATION

JD, Marquette University, Milwaukee, WI, 1987

BA, Business Administration and Political Science, Linfield College, McMinnville, OR, 1978

Bar Admissions: US Supreme Court, Oregon, Idaho, Washington, Colorado

HONORS AND AWARDS

Recipient of the Regional Industry Leadership Award, 2007

Certificate of Merit for Exceptional Performance, Centura Health, 2009

Certificate of Merit for Exceptional Performance, Centura Health, 2008

Certificate of Merit for Exceptional Performance, Centura Health, 2007

Certificate of Merit for Exceptional Performance, Centura Health, 2006

Board of Directors Chair, March of Dimes, Colorado Chapter, 2007

Board of Directors, American Cancer Society Chapter, serving 2005–2009

Board Member, Colorado Liability Reform Coalition, 2004–present

Colorado Healthcare Executive Forum — established Colorado Chapter

RESUME: DIRECTOR — SEEKING CAREER ADVANCEMENT

John is in his early 40s, and he had been a client for a long time. After every career change he came back and we worked on his next move. He had finished his doctorate in education and obtained superintendent certification for public schools. He was ready to go after the Big Job. Getting hired for a superintendent position is challenging. You compete against people at least as qualified as you, if not more qualified. We felt John had the best chance pursuing smaller school districts. The downside was that there are only a few openings each year. John had gotten a job description of his current job and one for the superintendent job. We used these two documents to help create his final resume. It was a complex task — but it worked. He's now happily working as a superintendent, in a job he defines as "ideal" for him.

John McCuthen, Ed.D.

1 Main Street
City, USA 11111
123.555.1212 cell
name@verizon.net

CAREER OBJECTIVE: SUPERINTENDENT OF SCHOOLS

SUMMARY OF QUALIFICATIONS

Award-winning educational leader with proven track record in district administration, plus twenty-two years of experience working as principal, assistant principal, and/or teacher. Notable expertise, having contributed to the enhanced student learning experience, resulting in raising schools' test scores, making process and systems improvements, and facilitating teacher training, which delivered a higher quality of education for a diverse student population. Strengths include: strategic planning, personnel management and staff development, organizational skills, project management, budgets and finance. Recognized as a highly respected professional by board members, faculty, staff, parents, students, legislators, and community members.

PROFESSIONAL EXPERIENCE

Director of Curriculum and Student Learning, Quincy School District, CA, 2005–present

Administrator, Quincy High School District, CA, 1996–2005

(Assistant to Superintendent — one year; High School Principal — six years; Assistant Principal — two years)

Principal, McKnight Middle School, Redding School District, 1992–1996

Teacher, High School, Redding, CA, 1986–1992

Instructional Leader

• Managed school district's instructional programs for three years. Responsibilities included: development of school improvement plans; working with principals on developing and implementing their school improvement plan; acting as district assessment coordinator;

developing and monitoring district learning improvement initiatives; overseeing district's information systems; leading initiatives on math/science program improvements district-wide; monitoring student academic progress at elementary/middle/high school levels; coordinating staff development/ professional growth programs; researching/selecting/adopting instructional materials; collaborating with regional partners/principals/teachers to create instructional best practices for subject-matter curricula district-wide; advising the home school and alternative program; handling district projects; plus assisting with staff selection and work assignments.

- Planned, analyzed, and implemented improvement plans to make adequate yearly progress as defined by the "No Child Left Behind" regulation, including: reviewing test scores; researching trends and demographics; discerning student achievement; advising principals on policy, student learning plans, resources; liaison to consultants and trainers; strategizing specifics on providing services with limited or no budget increases; and monitoring high school graduation requirements.

- Researched new initiative on differentiated instruction. Led year-long parent/teacher committee analyzing learning program options for gifted, middle, low, and mainstreamed students. Currently implementing the adopted initiative on differentiated instruction.

- Co-developed new district-wide comprehensive post-secondary student guidance and planning program. Curriculum model has been adopted by state as *Navigation 101.*

- Conducted complex research analysis evaluating district achievement and testing trends, comparing district patterns to state and regional trends. Analyzed data. Developed new learning initiatives and achievement targets, plus instituted staff training and in-service sessions to meet new goals.

- Managed the new/beginning teacher and professional certification induction programs designed to support teachers. Oversaw training process, offered individualized training, plus coordinated an assigned mentor program to foster new and beginning teacher success with better classroom management. Implemented programs with new policies and teacher training to reduce teacher attrition. Worked with principals to coordinate new administrator training.

• Researched ethnicity and poverty income level effects on learning trends, defining patterns, and notable educational models to develop strategy and best practices for school and district implementation.

• Developed and implemented the strategic plan for a comprehensive high school to achieve annual progress meeting the "No Child Left Behind" requirements, resulting in improvements that met goals.

• Implemented an innovative teacher evaluation system based on individual performance and growth. Program was a complete paradigm shift from old system. Results made teachers responsible for their professional growth and performance.

- Worked with technology staff to implement advancements and three-year technology plan.

Finance/Budgets/Operations

- Acted as a project construction manager for school campus with 20 buildings, 144,000 sq. ft. renovation project, while campus remained occupied. Conducted comprehensive needs analysis. Managed the design and plan development process with architects, contractor, and district/school representatives. Upgraded technology and equipment. Served as district building construction site supervisor. Coordinated numerous changes and resolved problems during two-year, $10 million building project.

- Worked as a district representative on the levy and bond campaigns.

- Developed in partnership with Superintendent innovative strategies to increase the district's end-fund balance. Analyzed spending patterns and contractual services. Studied procedures that decreased operational expenses; streamlined purchasing procedures; and made numerous process improvements.

- Assisted the Finance Director and Superintendent in management and development/adoption of annual multi-million-dollar general fund budget.

- Assisted with district budget, collaborating with transportation, food service, payroll, A/P, and contracted services.

- Planned and implemented large school district's emergency and safe schools plans.

- Oversaw the district's curriculum and professional development budgets.

- Worked on budgets, bargaining, and negotiations with the Redding teachers union.

- Wrote numerous state and federal grants. Received dozens of awards. Oversaw all grant management and compliance evaluations.

- Conducted comprehensive analysis of state's organizing and financing of public schools to determine best practices and strategies to maximize state funding.

Policy/ District Community Relations/Board Advisory

- Worked with Superintendent to plan school board meetings and handle communications with members.

- Developed strategies and activities to lead and operate the school district in compliance with current district, state, and federal policies, laws, and regulations.

- Advised school district board members on school district governance, vision, structure, accountability, including legal responsibilities.

- Made numerous formal presentations and reports to the school board and community groups.

- Researched and evaluated other regional school board meetings, processes, and operations. Developed/implemented best practices for school board operational management.

- Contributed to the school board's process in drafting and updating the district's strategic plan.

- Served as communications director and as author and editor of district's quarterly community newsletter. Improved coverage of educational reform projects, school and district news.

- Generated new publications, marketing materials, educational brochures, press releases. Enhanced the district's employee recognition program.

- Co-authored the "School Board of the Year" nomination application process that resulted in winning the "School Board of the Year" for the Redding District.

- Established improved parental, student, and community communications. Developed partnerships with civic, business, and religious leaders. Worked closely with booster clubs and PTAs. Oversaw extracurricular program development. Managed school and community activities. Worked on numerous community committees and enrichment projects. Improved relationships to increase support and endorsement of the schools.

• Acted as liaison for district and schools working to advocate public policy with state and local governments. Initiated numerous programs involving state recognition of school programs; hosted visits from legislative leaders (U.S. senators, state representatives, governmental officials); built partnerships with legislators to influence both educational policymaking and budgeting.

• Mentored teachers, counselors, coaches, and staff to interact more effectively with parents and the community at large.

• Two-year coordinator of district outdoor education program.

School Administration

- Served as principal for secondary schools with demanding socioeconomic and educational needs. Strategically hired teachers and staff to better achieve state learning goals. Fostered team and teacher development. Implemented new curricula. Organized staff and teachers training and in-service programs. Managed budgets. Redefined school department heads' and committees' roles.

- Served as assistant principal responsible for setting and implementing discipline policy for challenging school population. Served as liaison to probation officers, foster parents, social workers, and police. Supervised the special needs and special education programs. Established safety policies. Provided mediation and conflict resolution. Supervised building security. Handled daily operations. Supervised and evaluated numerous employees from different bargaining groups.

- Managed the classroom instruction with state mandates for learning objectives. Implemented curriculum, texts, materials, plus realigned scope and sequence. Managed and facilitated all teacher training and in-service programs on new curriculum development, instruction, and assessment.

EDUCATION AND CREDENTIALS

Ed.D., California State University, Long Beach, 2009

Initial CA Superintendent Certificate, included a two-year, two-thousand-hour Superintendent internship; completion June 2009

M.Ed., Educational Administration, Western Washington University, Bellingham, WA

B.A. Ed., English and Social Studies, Western Washington University, Bellingham, WA

Cum Laude Undergraduate Honors

HONORS AND AWARDS

Participant in ESD189 Superintendent

Academy, 2005–2006, 2006–2007

Examiner, Washington State Quality Improvement/Baldridge Award, 2005–2007

Board of Directors, Kiwanis, 2007–present

Recognized by OSPI for High School Achievement, 2004

Board of Directors, Career and Technical High School, 2004–2005

Chair, Legislative Committee, Association of CA School Principals, 2003–2004

Past President, County Principals League Association, 2000–2001

Executive Board Member, CA Interscholastic Activities Association, 1998–2000

Conference Presenter for Association of CA School Principals, 1992–2003

District Facilitator, Smith Center for

Leadership and School Reform, 2003

Excellence Award, CA Association of Supervision and Curriculum Development, 1999

Federal Recognition Award for Special Education Program Excellence, 1999

County Professional Certification Advisory Board, 2005–2008

RESUME: NURSE — RETURNING TO WORK

Mary was 51 and she hadn't worked as a nurse in fifteen years. When her husband got sick, they needed some income, so she returned to school for a refresher course and renewed her nursing certification. The resume she sent to me was so old it was typed on a typewriter. It was simply unacceptable and had little useful information on it except the employer names and dates of employment. At first Mary found a temporary job two days a week while she looked for something better. She had a lot of volunteer administration experience, plus experience as a nursing supervisor, but that was fifteen years old. We combined both paid and unpaid experience to target a higher-end administration position. Because she had been out of the workforce so long, we spent extra time perfecting her interview skills. Mary was thrilled when she landed a hospital nursing supervisor position, allowing her to restart her career at $62,000.

Mary Hilimire
1 Main Street • City, USA 11111
123.555.1212 cell • name@verizon.net

CAREER OBJECTIVE: RN POSITION

SUMMARY OF QUALIFICATIONS

Eleven years in direct-care nursing and nursing administration with a proven track record of leadership and innovative program development and process improvement. Well-organized with extensive project management and team-building expertise. Extensive hands-on patient care experience in Medical, Surgical, and Urgent Care areas, with an emphasis on providing high-quality, compassionate patient care. Terrific problem solver. Demonstrates exceptional oral and written communication skills. Known for being an instrumental team leader, effectively coordinating communications between staff, physicians, administrators, patients, and families.

PROFESSIONAL EXPERIENCE

RN, Urgent Care, Lakewood Clinic, NJ,

2007–2008

School Advisory Board/Community Program Development/Program Management, nonprofit organizations, 1995–2007

School of Nursing Director, Frankford Hospital, PA, 1987–1989

Nursing Program Manager, Lakewood Hospital, OH, 1987

Head Nurse/Nurse, University Hospital, Cleveland, OH, 1978–1985

Management/Program Administration

- Ten years of leadership roles in healthcare organizations and nonprofits providing program management, healthcare administration, budget management, program development, quality improvement, quality care best practices, delivery assurance.

- Created publications/brochures/reports; co-authored articles; edited and revised nursing medical textbook.

- Established and implemented policies, procedures, processes, and operational systems, staffing, supervision, staff training.

- Developed new scheduling model adapted for University Hospital nursing staff that improved staff workload equity, job satisfaction, and team morale.

- Planned, developed, and implemented a comprehensive six-week orientation program for new employee staff nurses for University Hospital. Results improved nursing performance and directly improved quality of patient care.

- Conducted in-depth analysis of hospital medical unit to evaluate problems, determine needs, review budgets, and assess protocols and floor operations.

- Created and implemented a strategic plan to improve operations and establish best practices; implemented new nursing protocol changes; organized staffing responsibilities and schedules; and provided in-depth nursing staff training. Results improved operations and improved job satisfaction and retention.

• Acted as project management leader overseeing numerous staffing, operations, community outreach, and program development projects. Responsible from conception through completion for all milestones, follow-up, and tracking to deliver on time and within budget.

• Designed a special program for studying the nursing needs, recruitment and retention programs for hospital's nursing staff. Organized off-site focus groups for data collections. Facilitated the five group sessions of nurses over two-day period. Evaluated and co-wrote hospital's final 60-page report with detailed findings.

Nursing

• Eleven years of nursing and supervising nursing staffs in urgent care and medical/surgical areas with nursing responsibilities including: patient care; pre-op/post-op care; administering medications; patient triage; staff supervision and scheduling; communications with patients and families; patient and family teaching; documentation; taking patient history; assessing patient status; nursing diagnosis; monitoring patient status; handling nursing procedures; development of care plans; and delivering clinic patient monitoring and care.

• Provided years of top-quality patient care recognized by superiors for displaying competency, empathy, compassion, and seamless teamwork.

• Provided nursing staff supervision and training for two floors of RNs and LPNs. Handled scheduling; budgeting; policy implementations; floor operations management; personnel evaluations; conflict resolution; dispensing referrals; and coordinating with physicians.

COMMUNITY LEADERSHIP HONORS

PTA President, High School,
Spokane, WA, 2001–2002

Community Center Board President,

Spokane, WA, 1993–1994

EDUCATION

Master's Degree in Nursing, University of Illinois, Chicago, 1987

BS, Nursing, New Mexico State University, Las Cruces, 1978

LICENSES

Registered Nurse — New Jersey — status: current

RESUME: PROFESSIONAL — SEEKING INTERNAL PROMOTION

Daniel, age 50, was a programmer and software engineer in a lead position, working for Oracle, when HR talked to him about a potential promotion. He had no resume at all, but he needed one to be considered for the promotion. He found a very brief, half-paragraph job description, so that's what we started with. Since it was an internal resume, this one could be more specific to the company, using its own acronyms and technical jargon. This resume went to a couple of area managers inside Oracle, and it got him an interview with each manager he sent it to. Daniel was pleased with his success — he secured a nice salary increase and a promotion with a new title.

Daniel Ting

1 Main Street • City, USA 11111

123.555.1212 cell • name@verizon.net

CAREER OBJECTIVE: SOFTWARE DEVELOPMENT ENGINEER IN TEST

SUMMARY OF QUALIFICATIONS

Proven track record as a software engineer leading teams working on OEMs and device driver development for twelve years. Broad expertise in software, firmware, and hardware development. Extensive experience collaborating with internal and external customers to troubleshoot and deliver innovative solutions. Display excellent oral and written communication skills, successfully working with technical and nontechnical personnel.

PROFESSIONAL EXPERIENCE

Lead Engineer, Oracle Corporation, Pleasanton, CA, 2007–present

• Worked as a software engineer dealing with Windows device drivers and services for twelve years, the last four as a lead engineer with Microsoft DDK Developer Support division.

- Demonstrated advanced-skill-level programming using C/C++.

- Wrote hundreds of thousands of lines of code and Windows kernel device driver development utilizing various data structures including lists, trees, graphs, and geometric algorithms.

- Led a device OEM driver engineering team. Provided analysis and consulting expertise to customers. Delivered solutions.

- Trained the customers' internal engineers and provided on-site developer support as needed.

- Led weekly project management meetings working with cross-functional teams dealing with storage, VDS, and VSS teams.

- Collaborated with customers and cross-functional teams, troubleshooting technical problems, handling debugging, and analyzing OEM systems.

- Conducted data analysis using probability and statistical methods.

- Made numerous product improvements for internal kernel components including: storeport, scsiport, LDM, VDS, and VSS.

- Gave technical presentations at the WinHEC convention and at TechReady 2007.

Technology Skills

Languages: C, C++, Perl, Ada, Assembler, Fortran

Operating Systems: Windows NT, Linux, VxWorks

Work History

Senior Software Engineer, Polyserve, Inc., Beaverton, OR, 2004–2007

Principal Software Engineer, NEC Systems, Inc., Redmond, WA, 1999–2004

Software Engineer IV, Phillips Medical, Inc., Redmond, WA, 1995–1999

Software Engineer, Boeing Company, Seattle, WA, 1992–1995

EDUCATION

BS, Physics, University of Washington, Seattle, 1990

EXTRA HELP IS AVAILABLE

For more samples, a guidebook, and detailed resume-writing guidelines, check out my book *Winning Resumes* (second edition), available at my online store at WWW.ROBIN RYAN.COM.

One of my services is resume and cover letter writing. Find out more about this personalized service by calling (425) 226-0414 or visiting WWW.ROBINRYAN.COM.

On my website you can take a resume quiz to see if yours will stand out from the crowd. Find it under "Quizzes" at WWW .ROBINRYAN.COM.

CHAPTER 13
EYE-CATCHING
COVER LETTERS

"Don't just wish for it, work for it and
make it happen."

ROBIN RYAN

Want to stand out from the crowd? Decision makers say: *write an excellent cover letter.*

People are getting lazier and aren't bothering to write a cover letter anymore. And if they do use one, it's usually too generic, written to fit any job they apply for. Your first sentence should capture an employer's attention and make him or her eager to learn more about you. It needs to be concise and point out your top accomplishments and the skills and experience you have that are necessary to perform the job you are applying for. Employers report they use the cover letter as a measuring stick to evaluate your communication skills, so composing a customized letter that is well written and carefully proofed is essential.

In our surveys, more than 90% of job hunters start their cover letters like this: *I'm writing to respond to the Sales Account Manager position I saw online.*

The hiring manager will probably stop reading if you use this introduction and just quickly glance at your letter and lightly scan the resume. Your goal must be to quickly explain how valuable you can be in meeting their needs and requirements.

A different approach will get you a lot further. The formula I use when creating cover letters for clients had a 96% success rate with the six hundred hiring managers we surveyed. You get attention with a strong first sentence, followed by a powerful paragraph. Employers repeatedly say they prefer this style. Here's an example of an opening sentence that grabbed the decision maker's attention. It resulted in a phone call to this executive the very next day:

I'm a results-driven senior sales executive with a proven track record in leadership and new business development, having delivered over $125M in increased sales revenues for my previous company.

Notice the difference? The most important part of your cover letter is that first sentence and paragraph.

The typical approach many candidates use only tells the DM what job they're applying for. In the above example, you told them *what you are bringing to the job.* It immediately tells employers you've got the skills that they're looking for. You are showing them how your skills will benefit them. You capture their attention, and they *will read* your letter. The subsequent paragraphs should be enticing and short, stressing only the necessary accomplishments to make your point. You don't need a great volume of information in the letter — that's what your resume is for. Use the cover letter to highlight specific experience important to performing the position.

Your first sentence should emphasize one, two, or three of your greatest strengths and summarize what you'd bring to the job. This typically will be the years of experience, special skills, and most importantly, previous accomplishments. Make your most important selling points in the first two paragraphs.

Keep your cover letter succinct — only one page. Most employers won't take the time to read a long letter. While your resume gets a fifteen-second glance, your cover letter gets maybe ten! The goal of your cover letter is to whet their appetite, tease them with what you've got to offer, get them to more carefully review your resume, and entice them to call you in for an interview.

APPLYING WHEN YOU'RE OVERQUALIFIED

Decision makers said that they see a huge red flag anytime someone over 40 applies for a job for which he or she has too much experience. They definitely notice if the job they are offering is a demotion. And they question: does this candidate really want *my* job? Or: is this just an act of desperation? On your end, often it is — after all, you need a job, and when the weeks turn into months of looking, any job will do. Unfortunately employers don't see it that way.

When an employer is looking at your qualifications and the cover letter says you want a middle management job, but the resume says in your last position you were a vice president, the hiring manager gets nervous. He or she wants to know *why* you are willing to take a job below your level of competency.

"No one seeks to hire their own replacement," one decision maker pointed out.

"It's a mistake when the person is overqualified and he or she doesn't address *why* they would want to change direction for a particular job." HR administrators look more hesitantly at you as an applicant when the job is obviously way under your skill level. Some said they automatically discard your resume when you are overqualified.

SOLUTION: The better option is to resolve this concern by eliminating it altogether. The higher you've advanced in your field, the fewer the opportunities, *but* it's better to search for a job at your own level. That means look harder, broaden your search, and expand to related fields. Although you may feel there aren't enough jobs to go after, spend your time carefully constructing the best cover letter and resume possible. Then look at your network to locate someone who either works for this organization or knows someone there, anyone who can help you pass on your resume internally. On the plus side, the job will be more interesting and the salary more appropriate. This strategy truly solves the problem by not creating it in the first place.

If you do have a valid reason to seek a lower-level position, better note why. Maybe you've been an independent consultant or had your own business that is struggling or failing. You could respond by saying something like this:

I love doing systems analysis but I dislike all the time away from that phase of the work to run the business, especially marketing myself. That's the reason I want to return to a corporate position so I can do what I love all the time: work on network systems.

Another angle: if you want fewer management duties, or less travel or commute time, address the issue with this example:

I've led sales teams for the last five years. That's a terrific job, *but* the amount of travel has been too hard on my family. I enjoy the selling and spend a lot of my time in the field doing just that. It seems like a natural fit to return to being a sales rep, especially with a local territory.

This person gave a valid reason, instead of scaring the DM into worrying about whether the applicant is after his job. You must seem enthusiastic and sincere in your desire to move into this lower-level job.

Be careful not to say you are looking for a "less stressful" or "low-pressure" job. Many employers worry that this translates into a burned-out employee who'll not be productive on the job. State that you would be happy performing the job advertised. If you won't, don't apply. You'll save everyone a lot of headaches, especially yourself.

EMPLOYERS' ADVICE ON WRITING A COVER LETTER

When asked, employers had strong opinions on how to either impress them or get your resume tossed into the circular file (a.k.a. the trash can). They expect more from the over-40 candidate. They assume you have acquired excellent communication skills after years of work experience. The cover letter is the very first thing the employer sees. Candidates who stand out use short, powerful statements, with sentence after sentence detailing past achievements. They note the talents and contributions they would bring to the new company or organization they are applying to. Many employers repeatedly said that for older candidates, the cover letter is *more influential than the resume,* because it is a truer sample of the candidate's communication skills, since they assume most candidates likely write the letters themselves.

Here are some of the decision makers' observations for the over-40 candidate, along with some insights on exactly how you can improve your letter and make it stand out and be noticed.

- **EMPLOYER SAID:** "I'm convinced when I read a poorly written cover letter, or one that is so generic it's like a form letter going out with every application, that the applicant can't write, is just lazy, or both."

  SOLUTION: Specifics sell — specifics and facts in the content of your letter are essential. Accomplishments and evidence of your productivity are the necessary ingredients to a good cover letter.

- **EMPLOYER SAID:** "The cover letter is my first impression of the person. Professionalism, a good format, and the style of the letter influence me to *read more or not read it at all.*"

  SOLUTION: Make sure you pay extra attention to layout. Indeed, the visual appeal of the letter makes an important difference and is influential. Do not use tiny fonts — keep the letter to one page, edit it, and only discuss a few crucial points to capture interest.

- **EMPLOYER SAID:** "The best way for someone to impress us is to address how all of the qualifications in the opening will be met by the candidate. Spell it out for me, succinctly!"

SOLUTION: Pick the major points you believe are essential to performing that job and address these by offering your experience or skills to excel in that position. If you are missing one qualification, such as a bachelor's degree, but have great experience, stress all the accomplishments and still apply, ignoring the educational requirement. In many cases, employers prefer *proof* of past success over a college degree that was earned twenty or thirty years ago.

- **EMPLOYER SAID:** "People fail to address the specific job they are applying for — you need to be clear on what position you want. After 40, you'd better know."

SOLUTION: Employers immediately

disregard an applicant who doesn't apply for a specific job — that means a *clear job title.* It's virtually impossible to get hired if you don't specify this and then use the body of the resume to show your relevant experience. After you are 40, employers expect you to know what you want from your career. Changing into a new area is fine, but you must be clear on what your specific goal is, and not hope they'll figure out where you'll fit into their organization. Your job is to tell them exactly how you will perform a specific job.

- **EMPLOYER SAID:** "I've changed the way I go about hiring people in the last three years. I used to rely heavily upon trying to find an applicant who met the requirements of the job description with the previous history and specific skills. Now I identify people who have a real passion to work in our industry and who can imagine possibilities for how the job might unfold. What scores points with me now is resourcefulness, creativity and imagination, flexibility, being a team player, ability to cope with change, and willingness to try new things. When you offer to bring your professional desire, passion, talents, and previous accomplishments, you've got a winning combination."

SOLUTION: Many employers look at the over-40 worker with a different lens. They look for leadership in terms of your being able to get the job done but also in being able to learn and grow into the worker the employer needs tomorrow. In our global economy, being productive, resourceful, and a great problem solver — showing initiative to find better ways — gets noticed. That gets the employer interested in you over the competition — fast.

- **EMPLOYER SAID:** "Your cover letter carries a lot of influence with me. A well-written letter can grab an interview just on its own merit."

SOLUTION: Customizing is the key. You must address the employer's needs.

- **EMPLOYER SAID:** "People try everything to get attention — hand-delivering it, sending it FedEx, using colored fonts and papers, sending a picture, using graphic designs, etc. It's usually to cover up a lack of substance or minimal skills with few accomplishments. It doesn't work — I am never impressed."

SOLUTION: Nothing will replace a simple letter with solid facts focused on how you can excel at performing the job. It's the "meat" of proven experience, skills, and accomplishments that truly gets attention and keeps the employer's interest long enough to call you in for an interview.

- **EMPLOYER SAID:** "Don't oversell. I see a lot of puffed-up statements being a national sales manager. Candidates offer grandiose statements like 'terrific closer,' 'one of the top salesmen you'll ever hire,' 'I'm the best,' 'I can sell anything,' but when looking a bit further I see quickly these are all unproven claims without the substance of specified achievements to back up the statement."

SOLUTION: In a recent survey in *USA*

Today, 64% of executives were cited for misrepresenting (a.k.a. lying) about the level of responsibility they'd had and exaggerating their accomplishments. Employers check references, and more and more they verify degrees and stated results. Don't create exaggerations no one will believe. It's better to state the truth in a positive light and offer statements with facts you can back up — not just rhetoric.

- **EMPLOYER SAID:** "Forget the superlatives when writing your letter. We already know we're a great company. What we don't know — and want to know — is how you can add to our team."

  SOLUTION: Cover letters need to say a lot in only a couple of paragraphs. Use the space to tell the prospective employer the specifics of how you would excel at the job. State what you've done before that would be of benefit to them. Noting how much you want to work for them is definitely needed for nonprofits or special causes, but keep it to no more than a sentence or two.

ADDRESSING THE REQUEST
FOR SALARY INFORMATION

Never send salary demands if you can help it. A significant number of hiring managers said they were downright offended when no salary information was even requested but a job applicant sent in their desires. Many noted that people actually write in saying, "I need $75,000 per year, plus full medical, dental, and retirement benefits." Or "I'm currently making $150,000." One hiring manager revealed how most felt about this, saying, "Some people send us a clear message that they are totally focused on their own needs and not on what they can do for our company, so we immediately delete them from the competition. We continue to look to find a better team contributor to interview."

If requested to send a salary history — don't. Ignoring it is your best option to preserve your salary negotiation power. Wait until *the job offer has been made* before you discuss salary. Hiring managers begin interviews to screen people out. Not until they have decided you are the person for the job do they then switch gears and begin to recruit you to take the position. It's only then that they fear you won't accept their offer. *This* is when you have greater power to get paid a higher salary since the DM is convinced you are worth it.

About a quarter of employers request a salary history. They use it as a measuring stick to assess your real skills, citing that a lower salary is more accurately reflective of a lower skill set. So you may lose out not because your salary demand is too high, but because your current salary suggests your skills are too low for the level of job being offered. Decision makers *assume* you overstated your results, when in fact your last employer underpaid you.

When a job ad asks you to send your salary requirement and states that they *will not consider you without your salary requirements,* then use this strategy. Do the research to find a reputable source you can cite that tells a salary range for your industry. For example, an attorney might say: "The California State Bar Association notes that a general counsel lawyer with over fifteen years' experience has a salary range of $175,000–$300,000, and I'm within that range." It's broad enough for you to negotiate within and it satisfies the stated requirement.

To learn exactly what your experience is worth, use our salary tools to find

out, at WWW.ROBINRYAN.COM/
BOOKREADER.

CHAPTER 14
COVER LETTER
GUIDELINES AND FORMATS

"Having high expectations for yourself is
the key to a wonderful future."

ROBIN RYAN

Never forget what is constantly running
through the employers' minds when they
seek a new employee. From the chairman
of the board to the line supervisors, they all
are thinking one thing when they look at
your cover letter and resume: *can this applicant do the job?* The first order of business in your cover letter is to assure them
that indeed *you can!*

Style, format, design, clarity, and conciseness — these are key elements in writing
your cover letter. But there are also a few
mistakes that are simple to avoid. A common one, a human resource VP wrote to
say, is a cover letter that has *no address,
email, or phone number* on it. They couldn't
contact this person even if they wanted to.

Assume your cover letter might accidentally get separated from your resume and be sure your complete contact information is on it. Also include any special designations, such as MBA, JD, PhD, or CPA, as these are a vital credential employers want to know about. Instead of writing "Kathy Joyce," it's more powerful to have your top line read "Kathy Joyce, MBA."

When creating your cover letter, keep your letter to *one page,* and do not use microscopic type. The letter must be easy to read, which means no small type. Keep the font clean — Arial is the font I use — size 12 point.

OPEN YOUR LETTER
WITH A STRONG STATEMENT

In my book *Winning Cover Letters,* I call this style of cover letter the Power Impact Technique. It is a two-step process in which you:

1. Analyze the job — both the noted and the assumed needs — and determine the most important skills the employer is looking for.
2. Immediately address how you will meet the employer's needs.

Begin your letter with a *strong opening sentence* that emphasizes the major selling points and skills you would bring to the job. Here are a couple of opening sentences taken from client cover letters that earned them a job interview:

- Ten years of senior management experience with proven expertise in international purchasing for a Fortune 100 company . . .
- A proven track record for delivering a 23% increase in fundraising revenues . . .
- Eight years of experience in student services program management within a college setting . . .
- Strong retail store management experience with proven expertise to improve sales, enhance the customer experience, and motivate employees.

As you can see, these openers are eye-catching, designed to get the employer to really read what you can do. The secret lies in simply addressing their needs right up front. After all, these are the necessary skills and experiences they are seeking.

The body of your letter is used to demonstrate proof that you can perform the duties desired. To develop this "proof," make an outline of the important points that the employer wants. Just underline the major items from the job opening announcement if you have one. Whenever possible, use your network to gather any inside information on what's most important to that employer for that job.

The next step is to ask yourself: *what were the* results *of my efforts on previous jobs, projects, or tasks that I've undertaken?* There's the key to composing your letter. Highlight the duties and skills needed by referencing your abilities to perform them. Offer any known results from your past efforts as the proof that you can do the job. Many of these points are simply shortened versions of content from your resume.

Conclude your letter with the power phrase: *I'd like to discuss in greater detail the valuable contributions I'd bring to your organization.* This shows you're productive and focused on being an asset to the employer. Also add your phone and email contact information.

Your cover letter must develop enough interest to get the employer to look at your resume and say, "Let's call this one in for an interview."

ELECTRONIC SUBMISSIONS

Today, more and more employers want you to paste your resume and cover letter into their software to apply. Some let you attach them to an email — as Paul (in the next chapter) did when he submitted his resume and cover letter. Here is an important strategy to follow when sending attachments. Create *one file* that contains your cover letter followed by a page break so your resume continues on the next page of that *single document.* Do not send two attachments. Don't assume they'll print out your email either. When you create it all in one document and attach that single file, it reduces the possibility that the employer might not open both files or put them together correctly.

More organizations are getting away from accepting attachments since it's the easiest way to get a computer virus. Also, when companies do advertise with an email, they often get hundreds of replies from candidates who have *no qualifications* to perform the job. Click and send is too easy. Do not think: *maybe the company will have something else available that will fit my skills.* This tactic is a waste of everyone's time because they are looking for a qualified applicant for *one specific* position.

Try to respond quickly when you see an opening. Many DMs admitted that they do not open every file they get, and once they find a few qualified applicants, they start scheduling interviews and the rest of the applicants never get a glance.

When asked to submit online, check to see if they have a place for your cover letter separate from your resume. If not, submit the one complete document with cover letter and resume together; "Copy" it all and "Paste" it in. You may need to adjust the format before you hit "Send."

If you are faxing your resume and cover letter to an employer, always test it first. Faxing can blur type, so making sure your font is easy to read and your contact information is clear, especially your email and phone number, is critical.

IMPORTANT TIP: Whenever possible also send a postal copy of your cover letter and resume to the hiring manager (or at least to HR). This gives you a double chance of getting noticed, and since many employers report that 35–40% of electronic applications are unreadable it's a useful safety precaution to give you a better chance to reach the decision makers.

The Format for Composing Your Letter Should Follow These Guidelines

1. Read the ad carefully to uncover the important needs stated by the employer.
2. Visit the website to learn more about the company and check to see if they have a more comprehensive job announcement.
3. Outline major points to stress in the letter.
4. Draft your opening paragraph and high-impact first sentence.
5. Write the body of the letter — decide if you will use short paragraphs or bullets.
6. Use the standard close.

Some letters use paragraph descriptions; some use bullets — either works well.

CHAPTER 15
COVER LETTER SAMPLES

> "Success comes from the faith
> in new possibilities and the courage
> to go after them."
>
> ROBIN RYAN

Note: All clients' names have been changed to ensure confidentiality. All other details are true and accurate as depicted in each cover letter and as seen by the employer.

Let's examine more closely how you use the Power Impact Technique to write an easy and highly influential cover letter. To begin, we must analyze the job this client was applying for:

JOB ANALYSIS

PRODUCT OPERATIONS MANAGER

People-to-People Ambassador Programs

Job Title: Product Operations Manager

Reports to: Senior Vice President, Product Management

Purpose: Responsible for implementing, scheduling, and reporting as well as budget tracking for two Ambassador Program International product lines: Leadership and Citizens Ambassadors.

Description of Essential Tasks:

- Assists with multichannel marketing campaign planning and budgeting.
- Coordinates work and communications cross-departmentally, assuring project quality, accuracy, and timeliness are met within agreed-upon budget parameters.

- Develops and monitors retention initiatives to improve overall delegate retention.
- Administrative responsibilities include:
  — Prepares project schedules
  — Tracks project progress and manages schedule
  — Tracks project budget
  — Reports status to product owners, management, and other stakeholders
- Other duties as assigned.

Candidates must have a BS/BA; 3–6 years of work experience; and previous time working in an operation or product management or product marketing environment. Operational or product management environment experience and people management and project management experience required. Candidates with cross-departmental project management experience preferred. This is a high-profile, developmental manager position providing a clear path for advancement opportunity.

Since neither I nor the client knew anything about this organization, she went to its website and learned it was an international program that arranged cultural experience trips for groups who wanted to travel to different parts of the world. That research gave her a better insight into this employer's needs.

Reviewing the employer's specific needs, program marketing, program management, and administration skills stood out. An added plus would be any experience working and organizing special events with people from different countries, as this was an international program. The client lacked a four-year degree. She did have great experience, so I encouraged her to apply anyway, as often employers will trade the degree for good experience in mature workers. Since this job was for a nonprofit, it was key also to stress her passion to perform this job and support the organization's cause. Here's the letter she sent to the employer, which got a quick response asking her in for an interview.

Tina McDonald

1 Main Street • City, State 11111
123.555.1212 cell • name@verizon.net

RE: Product Operations Manager position
Date

Dear Senior Vice President:

I'd bring a proven track record with ten years of experience in program management with strong marketing and administration skills to your Product Operations Manager position. It is programs like your leadership and citizen ambassadors travel program that truly inspire change globally. I believe the person-to-person experience is where the seeds are planted, and from there cultural acceptance and knowledge spreads. Your mission is truly an effort I could get behind, knowing I am making a difference.

I have had international economic development experience, and believe that all people everywhere are connected. I've worked with international delegates and travel. At TRADEC, which was an economic development organization (later bought by APCO), we recruited worldwide to get business delegates to attend our U.S.-based trade shows. I handled some of the communications and logistics and planned some travel excursions for delegates attending the conferences. Delegates came to Seattle from Asia and South America primarily.

I've managed numerous large-scale and smaller projects. I handled scheduling, budget management, regulatory compliance, operations, communications; plus conducted extensive collaboration with internal and external customers.

My marketing experience is strong and has an excellent prospecting and market research component of expertise. I have coordinated sales and marketing promotions, including special events, conferences, seminars, and educational sales events.

I pride myself on having delivered world-class customer service and built prosperous business relationships. I continually strive to exceed goals and expectations.

I would appreciate the opportunity to talk with you in greater detail about the valuable contribution I could bring to your team. I can be reached at 123.555.1212 or via email at: name@verizon.net.

Thank you for your consideration.

Sincerely,
Tina McDonald

Her closing is both positive and strong and reiterates her contact information. Indeed, within the week, this employer called her for an interview.

JOB POSTING

COMPANY: Microsoft

JOB TITLE: Localization Project Management

LOCATION: WA — Redmond

We are looking for an International Project Manager (long for IPM) who will share our responsibility to deliver Office to our customers in Japanese, Korean, and Chinese. The IPMs in our team wear many hats and own the process from end to end, starting with the localization plan per application all the way to signing off for the release. If you have 3+ years' experience in localization project management, and have a native level of Chinese abilities on top of that, we want to talk to you!

Responsibilities for this job include:

- Preparing localization strategies and plans and driving their implementation

- Working very closely with international teams and application teams across disciplines
- Managing vendor performance to reduce risk and costs and deliver on schedule
- Investigating and fixing localization issues and escalating as appropriate
- Troubleshooting automated systems in the localization process and suggesting improvements
- Delivering localized files to build and test teams on schedule

About the ideal candidate:

You are passionate about languages, curious to learn new things, have a minimum of 2 years' experience managing localization projects and localizing software UI in Chinese, are known for your excellent communication skills, are a very organized project manager, are sought out for your problem-solving and technical skills, have a flawless track record working with other teams, are creative and highly motivated, and are very proficient in Chinese.

Kim found the job listing at Microsoft but had applied there numerous times before and had no luck getting noticed. This time we created a much-improved cover letter, and he had a friend inside the company email it to HR. The HR recruiter called him within forty-eight hours after he sent it in — and yes, he did land this job.

Here is the cover letter Kim sent.

Kim Hwang
1 Main Street • City, NY 11111
123.555.1212 cell • name@verizon.net

Microsoft Corporation
Redmond WA
RE: Localization Project Management
Job Code: 37145
Date

Dear Microsoft:

As a native of China, I have five years of IT experience handling testing and client-server and database applications including Chinese language products. I was raised in China, but went to college in the U.S., and have worked for two U.S. companies here in Seattle since getting my B.S. in Computer Science from the University of Oregon. I really enjoy localization, and am interested in learning more about your International Project Manager position.

I had five years of experience testing Chinese and English versions of web-based applications. I worked on Chinese language products, and was responsible for ensuring that the Chinese user interface was correct and that the translation was accurate and appropriate.

My technical background includes managing projects involving enterprise software, infrastructure, and web-based applications. I was responsible for meeting milestones and deliverables and collaborating with team members. On certain projects, I was involved from the beginning and gave final approval to initiate release and launch of software and upgrades. My programming skills include Java, JavaScript, SQL, HTML, and XML.

I've been recognized for demonstrating superior communication and team development skills. I bring a success attitude to work each day and am dedicated to exceeding goals and expectations.

I would like to discuss in greater detail your current needs, and more extensively outline the valuable contributions I could make to your team. I can be reached at 123.555.1212 or email me at: name@verizon.net.

Your time and consideration are most appreciated.

Sincerely,
Kim Hwang

REGIONAL ACCOUNT EXECUTIVE

HIRING COMPANY INDUSTRY: Business Services

NUMBER OF EMPLOYEES: 10,000+ Employees

TOTAL COMPENSATION: $100k+

JOB DESCRIPTION:

We are a management organization competing in a billion-dollar industry in North America and provide an important service that really makes a difference.

ESSENTIAL QUALIFICATIONS:

- A sales professional with strong experience utilizing a complex, solution sales methodology.
- Ability to work with a Blue-Chip client list of Fortune 500 companies.
- Our client is a high-performance sales organization.

- Our client is one of only two global providers of career management services who can provide the type of international service that they can provide for their customers.
- Strong market share with a very profitable business model.
- An excited hunter with a proven ability to close new business; prior experience growing or building sales territories.
- Proven track record of taking business from competitors.
- Experience selling to "C" level executives as well as other senior leaders.
- A bright sales professional with strong business acumen.
- A collaborative team player.
- An aggressive sales professional with the ability to make or exceed quota, an overachiever.
- Undergraduate degree.

Susan was fired from her last position when the economy got tough and she was unable to make her former company's unadjusted sales goals. She did not want to move, so that limited her options. This job was posted by an executive recruiter so the company was not known. We addressed each qualification as carefully as possible and she submitted the letter below. It turned out to be an interesting job. This letter got Susan an interview, and she went on to accept the position, maintaining the $150,000 salary she made at her old job.

Susan Van Allen
1 Main Street • City, CA 11111
123.555.1212 cell • name@verizon.net

RE: Regional Account Executive
Position
Date

Dear Mr. Tripp:

I'm a results-driven senior sales executive with a proven track record in leadership and new business development, having delivered over $125M in increased sales revenues for my past employer, which briefly summarizes the background I'd bring to your client's Regional Account Executive position. I attribute some of this success to the consultative sales style I use to approach prospective clients and current customers. In my experience, it is the most effective relationship builder. I pride myself on developing mutually beneficial long-term relationships.

Some highlights of my background include:

- Led the regional sales team for multi-million-dollar sales consulting/training company, overseeing 13 states and Western Canada for seven years.
- Led sales team delivering over $180M of sales revenues during tenure.
- Managed team of four managers with 60 account executives selling office/computer products.
- Made sales presentations to VPs, EVPs, and C-level executives at mid-size, large, and Fortune 500 companies.
- Developed extensive new business by building key relationships that

doubled the region's sales revenues.

- Coached and trained sales team, working closely with reps to develop better sales skills.
- Made significant contributions as Sales Account Executive, moving from zero sales to be ranked fifth out of 20 account executives within 15 months.

I excel at collaboration and building superior customer relationships. I've been recognized for building highly productive teams that continuously exceed goals by delivering world-class service.

I would like to discuss in greater detail your current needs, and more extensively outline the valuable contributions I could make to your team. I can be reached at 123.555.1212 cell or via email at: name@verizon.net.

Your time and consideration are most appreciated.

Sincerely,
Susan Van Allen

Sometimes you get a lead but little other information to draw from. In this next client's case, there was no job opening posted. Paul got an email from a friend that said that a good company wanted a controller. No other information was available, so in his letter Paul hit on the major tasks he would perform in a controller job.

This letter did the trick — he got a call from the hiring manager and landed the first interview. He went on to have two more interviews, and he accepted the job at a nice salary increase over his old position.

Here is the cover letter Paul sent.

Paul Wheeler, CPA
1 Main Street • City, CA 11111
123.555.1212 cell • name@verizon.net

RE: Controller position
Date

Dear Company:

I'd bring ten years of experience as a controller with proven financial leadership managing a company's accounting operations to your Controller position. I have had experience in a large Fortune 500 company, as well as experience having led a midsized retailer that grew to 44 stores and doubled revenues during my tenure with them.

My previous responsibilities have included: financial statements; A/P, A/R; general ledger, cash flow management, taxes, banking, audit liaison, forecasting; budgeting, IT systems management, accounting and internal control functions; daily financial operations oversight; plus hired, trained, supervised, and coached direct and indirect reports.

As a controller, I have made numerous process improvements. I have streamlined and improved internal controls while raising the efficiency of the accounting department. I pride myself on providing excellent customer service to internal and external customers. I have a wide range of in-depth accounting knowledge and focus on personally developing my financial team to perform at the highest level possible.

I've been recognized for demonstrating superior communication skills. I frequently collaborate with other department managers, outside accounting auditors, and regulatory agencies. I bring a success attitude to work each day and am dedicated to exceeding goals and expectations.

I would like to discuss in greater detail your current needs, and more extensively outline the valuable contributions I could make to your team. I can be reached at 123.555.1212, or via email at: name@verizon.net.

Thank you for your time and consideration.

Sincerely,
Paul Wheeler, CPA

For additional examples, consult my book *Winning Cover Letters* (second edition), available at WWW.ROBINRYAN.COM.

■ ■ ■ ■

Part 4
INTERVIEWING
AND SALARY
NEGOTIATIONS

■ ■ ■ ■

"If you want to succeed and prepare to do so, you will achieve your dreams."

ROBIN RYAN

CHAPTER 16
WOW 'EM WITH A
SUCCESSFUL PRESENTATION

"Never underestimate the potential you
have to do more and be more."

ROBIN RYAN

You've still got a lot to offer any employer, and you know it. So leave nothing to chance. Instead, put in place two important strategies before you go off to the all-important job interview. These two strategies are very important advice for anyone over 40 because it's critical you make a terrific first impression.

That first interview, when you meet the decision maker or human resource director, or others on the hiring committee, must go well or someone else will get the job you are seeking. But before we begin your interview training, there are two key preparation steps to follow before you ever walk into the employer's door. These two strategies are:

1. Bring "proof" of past work that demonstrates your abilities and previous successes.
2. Be dressed as a vital, contemporary professional or executive.

SHOW AND TELL

One of the most influential things you can do as you approach your job interview is to have some real, physical examples of your past work. I refer to these examples as "show and tell" materials. Demonstrating the quality of your past work is the best way to paint a picture and communicate clearly to the DM that you will be a valuable asset in the new job. Bring items that represent how well you performed your previous job. Several possibilities exist.

For example, if you are a Web designer you'd bring in samples on a DVD of your past website designs, or take the employer to a website or two you worked on. A finance executive could bring in his laptop and show spreadsheets that illustrate budget reductions and how he saved his company thousands or even millions of dollars. He'd need to be careful not to share any trade secrets or proprietary information. This holds true for many executives. A marketing professional could bring in samples of marketing materials she created, things such as packaging, advertisements, flyers, brochures, or direct mail promotions. Do think it through and be careful in your selection if you are talking to a competitor of your own current employer. A C-level executive could bring in accounting reports showing profit and loss statements demonstrating his level of responsibility and showing how revenues increased under his leadership. Maybe you were a speaker at a professional event; then bring in an event brochure to show you are considered a leader in your field. A project manager could bring in a timeline that shows how she tracks complex projects to meet milestones and deliverables on time. A service professional could bring in a thank-you letter, full of praise, written by a customer or client. A communication specialist would want to bring in published writing samples, such as newsletters, articles, annual reports, or policies and procedures manuals he has written.

Bring some tangible items — preferably items that you can leave behind — that you've done for a previous employer. These can impress the DM and will serve to paint a picture that allows the employer to see you performing similar tasks successfully for his or her company. This physical evidence is very persuasive. It supports what you have explained during your interviews and helps convince the DM you are the right person to fill the open position.

In the course of your interview you'll find an opportunity to answer questions and, at the appropriate time, pull out your samples. You may also wait until the interviewer asks you related questions — then offer to show them and not just tell your story. When you offer specific details you make the employer think, "Yes, that's what we need." Using past work examples will go a long way toward supporting your suitability as a new employee. It is a memorable way to communicate.

PACKAGING IS AN IMPORTANT PART OF MARKETING YOURSELF

The front page of the *New York Times* website recently had an article entitled "Nice Resume: Have You Considered Botox?" The article asked readers if looking "old" was bad for their career. Pretty shocking, isn't it? Yet you'd be amazed at the number of DMs and HR professionals who said the over-40 population lives in a fashion time warp. They felt many looked out-of-touch and very old-fashioned.

A CEO for a $300 million organization

stated that she has hired hundreds of people and has seen many candidates come in — from C-level executives to administrative assistants — who are naively unaware about how outdated they look. The interviewer mentally crossed them off the hiring list before they said a word.

Another CEO summed it up nicely, stating, "There is a presumption that if your look is out-of-date, your information/skills and attitudes are also out-of-date. Most over-40 job hunters have not had a makeover in ages and don't realize how off-putting their appearance can be, especially to a younger interviewer or when they will be working with younger coworkers and/or customers!"

First impressions are critical. Your appearance must be professional, contemporary, and downright spectacular. You need to embrace this chance to meet the DM with a warm smile, eager enthusiasm, and a look that's as sharp and professional as possible.

Remember, you are marketing a product — yourself — to a potential employer, and the first thing the DM or hiring team sees before you say a word is your attire and personal presentation.

Our country is obsessed with a youthful society. Female models are young, beautiful, and incredibly thin, with flawless skin. Men in magazines are buff and handsome, with a full head of hair. Even when you see photos of older movie stars they look perfectly groomed and appear not to have aged a day in twenty years. It's an illusion. Thanks to cosmetic surgery, makeup artists, dermatology advances, and *a lot* of Photoshop fixes, their images have achieved perfection by the time they reach the magazine's pages.

When you are job hunting you can come face-to-face with your age and suddenly realize how others perceive you, based on age alone. Yet in your mind you feel the same as you did when you were thirty. It's only when you face the mirror you realize a lot of time has gone by.

Yet, as time passed, something else important happened. You grew in your job, became better educated, learned how to cultivate relationships, and made important business and personal contacts. Your leadership skills expanded. You gained greater expertise in your field or learned how to perform particular work tasks. You mastered things. You became the person others look to for answers. Aren't you a better worker now than you were five or ten years ago? Most people are. Decisions should not be based on the year you graduated from high school.

Your skills and accomplishments must be the primary criteria to determine whether or not you are qualified for a particular job. A professional image update may be necessary to help you stay in the running once they meet you in person.

LOOKING AS SUCCESSFUL AS POSSIBLE

Employers want to hire a person who can hit the ground running and get the job done. Vitality and enthusiasm are important, someone with an attitude of success that says, "I'm ready to deliver the results you need." These are the essential traits you must display when you are over 40. This approach will help you defy some common stereotypes that exist concerning mature workers. You can't ignore these "age" stereotypes, as they often derail candidates.

Accept that some hiring managers may suffer from preconceived ideas and believe some of the stereotypes about a reduced performance level in mature workers. The best way to disarm this prejudice is to prove them wrong.

Contemporary and stylish is the look you are after. *Fresh! Vibrant!* No drab colors. You want to look the very best you can, and definitely better than you might look on the average workday. Casual business attire is *not* impressive. It's just that — casual. You need to dress up as you would for an important presentation or if you were meeting with the company's board of directors, its top client, or a CEO. *Dress to impress* is your motto. But dress in something that has seen the light of day in the last year; not something you bought ten years ago.

Don't let something you can control — your personal attire and the way you present yourself — create a problem. Take steps to avoid looking "old" or outdated! You may think you are past the age where you need to dress to impress. Not true. Employers make snap judgments and you don't want your attire to turn them off and make them think your best work days are behind you.

Few of us are as fit and thin as we were in our youth. The effects of aging can be downright cruel and may crush our self-image. The side effects of medication, menopause, high blood pressure, and a sedentary lifestyle all add more pounds than most of us would like. Many people over 40 are overweight — some very overweight. Being able to easily drop fifty pounds while you are job hunting is a fantasy that isn't likely to come true. Diets and exercise go a long way to help you look better toned and more fit, but it will take a serious commitment, hours at the gym, and serious dietary changes to shed a lot of excess weight. It's commendable if you want to work toward this goal, but you must also make the most of how your body looks right *now*.

So what do you wear to an interview? What's appropriate in this day of casual business attire? What is old-fashioned? What is contemporary? How do you find out what is the proper dress for a given job/company/industry? If everyone is very causal should you dress the same way?

You could try to visit the organization before your interview to get an idea. Or ask insiders, or people in your network, what is appropriate at the place you have an interview. A good rule of thumb is *better to be safe than sorry.* Any job at the director level or higher requires a suit. That goes for many professionals as well. It's my recommendation for both men and women over 40 that a suit is almost always the correct interview outfit.

Key strategies that have helped clients look more vital and appealing to employers are broken down by gender below.

TIPS FOR MEN

You must look sharp at your next interview. Don't underestimate the importance of this. Go to WWW.ROBINRYAN.COM/BOOKREADER to see some before and after makeovers of men who dressed the way they normally would for a job interview, and then underwent a presentation update. You'll literally "see" the improvement. You can use these pictures as visual clues for how to make yourself look as good as possible.

Men over 40 need to recognize (or admit) that their physical attributes have changed. Changes in hair and skin color alter your appearance so it is essential to wear colors that are flattering.

- **BUY A SUIT THAT MAKES YOU LOOK TERRIFIC.** Go for the "classic" look, not too trendy. *Fit* is the important element here. Go to a tailor so you get a perfect fit. Shopping your closet is not a wise idea when you want to look contemporary — for most men, the suits have been hanging there for years. Be sure you don't resort to wearing something outdated — too small or too large: you will look old-fashioned and out of touch. *You must avoid that* *image!* Crisp, clean lines give you a polished look. Pick a color that complements your appearance — blues or grays usually work best.

- **SHIRT, TIE, SOCKS, SHOES.** Beige is a *bad color* for shirts. French blue, which is a rich medium blue, is a flattering color for most skin tones. It makes a great dress shirt. Others might look great in a shade of gray or with a subtle pinstriped dress shirt. On some men white Oxford shirts look fine, but as you age a stark white, stiffly starched shirt might give out the "I'm old!" message. Be careful the collar isn't too tight or that will add to the "old-fashioned" image you are trying to avoid. Ask a salesman in one of the higher-end stores, like Nordstrom or Brooks Brothers, to help you select a shirt color and contemporary tie that enhance your natural skin tone and hair. Avoid those loud and obnoxious theme ties — no colorful trout or sports logos! Socks need to be a plain dark color *matching the pants.* Finish off your appearance with dress shoes that are freshly polished. And — this is an absolute must — *clothes and shoes must be impeccably clean.*

- **ATTIRE IN A VERY CAUSAL ENVIRON-MENT.** Some places, especially high-tech companies, have a relaxed dress code. In this situation a nonexecutive might elect to go in a long-sleeved dress shirt, a tie, and dress pants. Shoes must be dress shoes — no sneakers. Keep the image on the higher end of professional no matter that people wear jeans to work daily.

- **GET A CONTEMPORARY HAIRSTYLE.** It will do wonders and take years off your face. Shorter, classic cuts are appropriate. Nothing too short — no buzz cuts — which really age men. Receding hairlines are a part of life. Accept it. If you have a bald head, don't try covering it with a few, wispy strands of hair; that looks worse, not better. As hair turns gray or white, some people use hair coloring as a temporary option. That can enhance your appearance during that all-important interview. So if it'll give you more confidence, go ahead, but get a professional to do it so you don't end up looking worse instead of better. Also, you may have multiple interviews so be sure to have touch-ups very frequently during this job search process.

- **FACIAL HAIR.** In employment studies, hiring managers reported that they preferred men who were well-groomed and freshly shaved. Facial hair, especially mixed with white or gray, generally makes men look older. If you have a mustache or beard, and it is turning gray, shaving it off, or dyeing it, will help you regain a more youthful appearance.
- **APPEARANCE ENHANCERS.** A worthwhile investment is to visit your dentist and get your teeth whitened. Nothing ages your face more than stained or yellowed teeth. Glasses can create a youthful effect or make you look dated. Go to the optical store to see what a new pair of frames might do to improve your looks, or consider contacts. Facials (yes, for men!) can help polish your skin and improve your appearance. If your skin has a lot of redness, age spots, or broken capillaries, a dermatologist can provide treatments that smooth lines and restore a more youthful skin tone. (While facials can help polish your skin and improve its appearance, be careful to allow several days between the facial and a job

interview in case redness or blemishes result.) Dieting and daily exercise can make a significant difference and give you a trimmer, more vibrant appearance. You'll feel better about yourself, and feeling better psychologically will give you a personality boost when you are searching for a new job.

- **HYGIENE MATTERS.** Before you meet an employer make sure nails are trimmed and clean; clothes are pressed and fresh; and you've showered before the interview. Wear unscented deodorant. Use cologne sparingly, if at all.

- **TABOOS.** Avoid loud designs, outdated or weird-colored suit jackets, flashy ties, patterned or mismatched socks, and ostentatious jewelry. Don't ask if it's okay to smoke (it's not) and don't go into the interview smelling of tobacco or alcohol.

TIPS FOR WOMEN

Instead of assuming that you come across just fine, it is much better to know you do. Go to WWW.ROBINRYAN.COM/ BOOKREADER to see some before and after makeovers of women who dressed the way they normally would for a job interview, and then underwent a presentation update.

You'll literally "see" the improvement. You can use these pictures as visual clues and style ideas for how to make yourself look as good as possible. You're going to want to do this in advance so you're armed with your outfit before any interview comes your way. That way there is no panic the day before trying to "find the right suit."

Aging typically isn't kind to women. One of the biggest criticisms DMs made about women over 40 was that they looked "frumpy." To them frumpy equals old, dowdy, out of touch, dull, and possibly not an ambitious worker. Sadly, if you dress in a frumpy manner, you begin to feel frumpy. If you feel frumpy, you start to act frumpy. When you act frumpy, it will show in your work, in what you say, and in the loud negative impression you'll make on the interviewer. Employers complained about women coming in looking tired and listless, so pay attention to your appearance to ensure that you look vibrant and contemporary. Think sophisticated, feminine, classy, and flattering. Most likely, the ideal outfit or business suit for your job interview is not hanging in your closet. Most things will be too casual or outdated. Banish anything that is too baggy, sexy, or sloppy-looking. You want to look stylish, up-to-date, and professional. To put your best self forward, here are some key guidelines to follow.

- **CHOOSE A FANTASTIC, FLATTERING SUIT.** Color is the key here. Many women know what colors and shades look best on them. Navy is a classic, but red, black, tan, purple, brown, or yellow might be a better choice, if it enhances your appearance. You want to look vibrant and full of life. Think stylish, conservative, attractive, but not too trendy. Don't go overboard with shimmering fabrics. Certain outfits will complement your skin tone and make you look slimmer (and thereby younger) simply by the color or cut. Something as simple as the hemline length can make you look older or younger. Play with hemlines to determine which length looks best on you. If you are unsure of what to wear, ask a fashionable friend to help you or visit a high-end department store and ask the salesperson for assistance. Here's a key fashion principle to follow: *make sure your suit is tailored to fit you.* Covering the less-than-perfect body requires a *great* fit. This is essential! Anything that is too tight or too baggy will scream "old lady." And visit the foundations department. You can smooth out your look with body-shaping undergarments that will help your clothes fit better and give you a more streamlined appearance. Some women are in great shape but forget that wearing anything too tight, sexy, or revealing is inappropriate. Avoid dressing in the latest teenage fads or twenty-something trends. Strive to look professional, and make your image very businesslike.

- **ACCESSORIES, HANDBAGS, SHOES, HOSE.** People do notice your purse and shoes. Wear dress shoes with moderate heels that are stylish and match the outfit you are wearing. A contemporary handbag adds to the polished look — be sure it's a current style. Keep your jewelry simple, with one exception: larger earrings, even those with a bit of sparkle, will bring the focus up to your face. Glance through fashion magazines to see if wearing neutral pantyhose, colored hose, or leg-tanner is in vogue, then select accordingly. If you wear glasses, maybe a new style is in order. Glasses have a big impact on how you look, and fashions change frequently. Go to the optical store to see what a new pair of frames might do to improve your look. And — this is an absolute must — *clothes and shoes must be impeccably clean.*

- **GET A CONTEMPORARY HAIRSTYLE.** Coloring your hair can take ten years off your looks. Not a bad investment of eight dollars. But before you experiment: if you aren't experienced at coloring your own hair, I recommend you go to a stylist who is a professional. Touching it up yourself will be much easier then, and an experienced stylist can make a tremendous difference in your appearance. Your hairstyle needs to be age appropriate and enhance your face. Avoid very short, tightly cut looks, overly teased, or heavily sprayed hair — all come across as old-lady-like. Very long hair that you've worn exactly the same way since high school doesn't work either. Wrong image! You want to look stylish and vibrant. You want to have hair that is nicely styled, flattering to your face, but age appropriate. Think sophisticated style. Adding highlights can solve the problem of uneven coloring, or if you are graying see a stylist about dyeing your hair or adding highlights so you will look more youthful. Always insist on high-quality products and get frequent touch-ups.

- **MAKEUP.** Every woman looks her best with a little bit of makeup. But wearing the same products you have used over the last twenty years most likely doesn't adjust for the fact that your skin tone and the shape of your face has changed. Skin becomes dry, dull, and lined and sometimes develops age spots. A good moisturizer and eye cream are the first essentials as we age. A trip to the makeup counter at a fine department store can be beneficial. Not only can their makeup experts give you a refreshing new look, but they can teach you tricks for applying makeup that will enhance your looks and brighten an over-40 face. Makeup manufacturers are always developing new products. Foundation can add years to your face if it's chalky and powdery looking. Try a lighter one (Giorgio Armani makes a great foundation for women past 40). Maybe a tinted moisturizer is all you need. When I suggested this step to one of my clients, she was skeptical, but she took my advice and went to the mall and tried on several products. She was so surprised to see the difference. The new light foundation she put on, in small amounts, indeed took years off her appearance. Mascara, and a bit of shadow to accentuate your eyes, enhances your look. Lipstick must not be too dark. Intense reds are taboo and anything in a dark shade tends to make you look older. Lips get thinner as we age, so use a neutral lip pencil to line and fill in the lips. Add a pretty shade of pink or coral lipstick to freshen up your face.

- **APPEARANCE ENHANCERS.** There's no shame in defying your age. A dermatologist can work wonders these days with laser treatments, fillers, and injectable products, but these procedures are costly. Only you can decide if these temporary time-erasers are something you want to consider. Many women who have had these procedures rave about them. You may want to check into it. Many women get facials and they are a great way to look better. While facials can help polish your skin and improve its appearance, be careful to allow several days between the facial and a job interview in case redness or blemishes result. A definite worthwhile investment is to visit your dentist to get your teeth whitened. Nothing ages your face more than stained or yellowed teeth. Glasses can have a youthful effect or make you look ancient. Go to the optical store to see what a new pair of frames might do to improve your looks. You already know that dieting and daily exercise make a big difference and can give you a trimmer appearance. Begin today to work toward that goal.

- **HYGIENE MATTERS.** Before you meet an employer, treat yourself to a fresh manicure. Make sure that all your clothes are cleaned, wrinkle-free, and fresh, and that you've showered that morning. Wear unscented deodorant and go *very light* on the fragrance, or don't wear any at all. Many people are sensitive to fragrance so it's safest not to wear it. You don't want to give your potential employer an allergy attack.

IMPROVING YOUR IMAGE
INCREASES YOUR SELF-ESTEEM

When you look good you feel better about yourself. Look at your reflection in the mirror and ask yourself: *do I look as good as I can today?* Smile at yourself and tell your reflection that you are ready to take on the challenge. When you know you look your best, you'll radiate a confidence that will charm any employer you meet.

Chapter 17
Acing the Job Interview

"Success is when opportunity
and preparation meet."

ROBIN RYAN

When you walk into the job interview, concentrate on what's going through the employer's mind. He or she hopes that you are "the one." The decision maker liked you enough, when reviewing your resume, to have someone call you to do a screening interview. Usually that's HR's job, but sometimes the DM calls personally.

The decision maker knows selecting the right candidate is a key decision. The DM has high hopes, before you arrive, and is pondering a few key questions.

- Can you do the job?
- Will you do the job?
- Will you fit into our company?
- Can we manage you?

Prove that indeed you are able to do the job, willing to do the job, adaptable, and manageable — *and* that your age is not a hindrance — and you'll get hired.

The interview is your big opportunity to sell yourself. Some are good at this, but in my experience, a lot of people are not. Many of you may have gone a long time without interviewing, so a refresher course is essential. I often do interview coaching and preparation with sales and HR professionals. While these clients excel in their jobs, many are very uncomfortable when facing a job interviewer. While you'd think they'd need no prep by the nature of their positions, in fact, people in these roles are frequent clients.

Anyone can improve with the right strategies. The key to answering even the toughest questions is to think and prepare answers *before the interview.* Practicing (especially role-playing) is important to help you get comfortable, and to adjust and perfect your answers.

You certainly need to *know what to say.* Many people over 40 get really nervous, and some freak out and stumble when they are asked hard questions. Following are some comments I've heard a lot from clients over the years. These may reflect some of your concerns:

- "I can't answer those questions about weaknesses."
- "I lost it when the interviewer said, 'I'm a little worried about your lack of experience with . . .' "
- "I seem to lose out when the employer says I'm overqualified, so why do I want this job."
- "I got fired from my last job so I don't know what to say when asked why I left it."
- "How do I explain why I've had so many jobs?"
- "I thought having only one employer for over ten years would be a plus, but employers seem turned off by it. What do I need to do?"
- "Employers see a big employment gap while I was at home with my kids, and I don't have anything to say beyond I was a great parent."

Advanced preparation will aid you in developing solid answers to these concerns.

THE 5-POINT AGENDA

Most employers can remember only a few specifics about each applicant they interview. The "5-Point Agenda" is a way to ensure that the employer will clearly remember five specific points about you once you depart from the interview. By selecting your top five selling points and weaving them into your answers throughout the interview, the employer will note and remember important information about you.

What are the five points that you want the employer to remember about you? Analyze what's most important in performing the advertised job and what you bring to the position, most notably: experience, strengths in certain areas, past duties that show you are qualified, plus any supervisory skills. Each point needs to be a key component to doing the employer's job. Closely analyze the information you have gathered about the employer's major concerns, things that you've uncovered during your research or from your contacts. Write out the specific duties you know are necessary to do the job. Then make your list of five major points. These five points are your self-marketing strategy. They'll focus you on presenting your best abilities to the employer during your interview.

To help you better understand this tool, here is an example of a 5-Point Agenda that Steve, a client applying for a VP position as head of stores, used in an interview. His 5-Point Agenda included:

- Point 1: Award-winning regional sales manager for national retail store chain.
- Point 2: Fifteen years of experience in retail management, marketing/sales, team development, and budgets.
- Point 3: Entrepreneurial drive.
- Point 4: A proven track record delivering major improvements in customer experience, in-store layout, merchandizing, and cost reductions, to deliver higher sales at each store.
- Point 5: Excellence at coaching managers and team members to higher levels of performance.

Eventually, as you move up in an organization, especially at a VP level or higher, you no longer get the job done alone. You must instead motivate others to get new strategies implemented and the work done. The inside information we had on this job was that they needed someone who could get results and Steve had a solid track record of doing just that.

Creating a 5-Point Agenda gives you a direction and navigation technique to focus your interview. Over-40 candidates need this tool to avoid being vague or offering too much information that is *not* relevant to performing the advertised job.

THE 60 SECOND SELL

The 60 Second Sell is a memorized statement that concisely summarizes and links together all the points in your 5-Point Agenda. It is a proven and effective way to clearly communicate to an employer the skills that you bring to a job. Take your five points and link them together into a few sentences. When spoken, it should take no more than sixty seconds. To better enable you to do this for yourself, here are the five points woven into Steve's 60 Second Sell:

I'm an award-winning regional sales manager, having worked for a national retail store chain with 185 stores. I spent six years as a retail store manager and increased the store sales by 31%. I bring an entrepreneurial drive to work each day. I took over the chain's worst territory and doubled sales revenues. I have a proven track record for delivering major improvements in customer experience, store layout, and merchandizing that resulted in delivering higher sales at each store. I do more with less. I can contain or reduce costs, decrease labor expenses, and reduce staff and manager attrition. I do this by consistently coaching and training both managers and team associates to higher levels of performance. They are the key to my success.

That actual 60 Second Sell helped Steve land the job. It helped him stay focused and overcome his tendency to add too many irrelevant things and to babble when answering questions.

You can stress any points you feel are going to be important. During the interview, when you are asked a question like "Why should I hire you?" or "Tell me about yourself," your answer is simply your 60 Second Sell.

Customize your 5-Point Agenda and 60 Second Sell for every job interview, based on a complete analysis of that job's needs. It takes time and effort, but it really works.

SITUATIONAL QUESTIONS

Behavioral interviewing is a style of asking questions to elicit examples of past behavior. *Situational questions* are synonymous with *behavioral interviewing.* These questions ask for specific details from a specific job. Employers consider how you behaved in your job in a similar situation in the past and see it as a predictor of how you are likely to perform in the future. These questions are indeed challenging. And you never know in advance who is going to use them.

This style of interviewing asks you to give specific examples of positive and negative work situations. These questions often start out with "Give me an example," or "Tell me about a time," or "Describe a situation." They seek details of your past abilities and performance. Then the interviewer rates each response to determine and predict your future performance with her company. These situational questions are thought-provoking ones. The interviewer is looking for specifics: specific details, specific illustrations. Practice answering these types of questions by giving concise, detailed examples. Candidates frequently find these questions very difficult.

Here is an example of this type of question and my suggested response.

"Tell me about a recent mistake you made at work where your boss corrected you."

KEY STRATEGY: In answering this question you must quickly establish the circumstances. Set up the scene with who, what, where. It is helpful to select something in which you went on to fix it, such as: "My boss criticized my spreadsheets, saying they were too simplified. Since Excel isn't a software application I knew very well, I realized she was right. I enrolled in two Excel classes, and now I do pretty sophisticated spreadsheets that have the comparisons and details my boss wants. She even mentioned that she noticed my improvement."

In this case you said there was a problem, and you took the initiative to learn new technology and advance your skills, which shows you are adaptable and will grow with the job.

DEALING WITH TOUGH, TRICKY QUESTIONS

There are four key components to successfully answering interview questions:

- Preparing in advance
- Giving short, concise, specific answers that never exceed sixty seconds
- Demonstrating ability to perform the job
- Exhibiting that you are engaged, focused, and interested in performing the job

Answering tough questions is easier when you've had time to contemplate them. Knowing what you want to say to answer the employer's questions is vital to your success. Your self-confidence is dependent on knowing you can effectively answer questions that demonstrate to the employer that you can do the job.

A good way to prepare is to write out answers to questions you might get asked. I recommend you review my book *60 Seconds & You're Hired!* before your interview. It is a comprehensive guide to the entire interview process. It provides answers to more than a hundred questions you may be asked during the interviewing, and it also covers salary negotiations in depth.

ILLEGAL PROBING

Employers are not supposed to ask you any questions about race, religion, marital status, disabilities, ethnic background, country of origin, or age. But the fact that these kinds of inquiries are illegal doesn't stop some interviewers from asking them anyway. Although asking "What country are you from?" is an illegal question, I suggest that you assure the interviewer and respond by saying, "I am authorized to work in the

United States."

When confronted with age questions it can be pretty tricky. When an interviewer asks "How old are you?" or "What year did you graduate from high school?" then you know your age is a real concern to them. By telling them you don't have to answer the question — legally you are within your rights to refuse — you'll likely come off as a confrontational and possibly problematic employee. The result is you will probably lose out on getting hired. To reassure the employer you can state your age in a more generic way, using a range such as "I'm 40-something" or "I'm in my mid50s." One 60-year-old woman told me she smiled her biggest smile and said, "Sorry, but a lady never tells her age." Everyone laughed and they moved on. If you elect to say "I graduated from high school in 1969," I suggest you then go on to state, "I've been fortunate to have such a successful career. I love my work, it engages me to solve problems, learn new things, and because of my experience I can often make major contributions." It'll get the interviewer past concerns such as "Is this person too old? Can she do the job? Does she have the drive or energy I need?"

Be very careful when they ask about the possibility of retiring. Employers worry that people near retirement are "dead on the job." Too often they have had "deadwood" as people wait to finish working for good. They are quite concerned that you need the paycheck but have checked out on contributing very much. Be sure to give examples of recent accomplishments and how you can perform their job well. Be vague if pushed about how long you plan to work. After all, sometimes you don't know for sure since you may work longer — or shorter — than you think.

PRACTICE QUESTIONS

Here are some common questions for job candidates over 40. Although it's possible an employer may not ask even one of them, more than likely he will ask several. No matter what, you will have thought through your answers and will be prepared for almost anything. This preparation will give you confidence, and that confidence will show.

First, think about what objections this employer might have. Try to weave into your answers facts to dispel any concerns that may be floating through the DM's mind.

Consider what she may be thinking; for example:

1. Does she think I'm too old?
2. That I am not flexible?
3. Does she feel I'm overqualified?
4. That my experience is too outdated?
5. Does she worry my computer skills are weak or very slow?
6. Why does she keep asking about recent accomplishments — are mine too old?
7. Is she wondering how easily I'll learn the new job or their industry?
8. Is she wondering if I have kids and if they will interfere with my job?
9. Is she worried that I'm stuck in my ways?
10. Does she think I'm not flexible, adaptable, or open-minded?

These are often unasked concerns. Although they are not voiced you do need to address them by weaving them into your answers. Here are some key questions — typical, difficult, and situational — you'll likely be asked. Prepare answers before you go into the interview.

1. Tell me about yourself.
2. Why did you leave your last job?
3. What is your greatest weakness?
4. What are your strengths?

5. Give me an example of how a co-worker would describe your personality.
6. Why should I hire you?
7. Tell me about your proudest accomplishments.
8. In what ways do you think you can make a contribution to our company?
9. Describe your ideal supervisor.
10. Describe yourself as a supervisor.
11. Describe your worst supervisor.
12. I'm worried about your lack of experience in . . .
13. Why haven't you obtained a job so far?
14. Describe how you work under pressure, with deadlines, in a fast-paced, high-stress environment.
15. What two or three things are most important to you in your job?
16. Why did you decide to seek a position with this company?
17. What do you know about our company?
18. Why have you changed jobs so frequently?
19. Will you relocate? Do you have any concerns or any reasons why relocation would be an issue?

20. What motivates you?
21. How much travel is acceptable to you, and what was your travel level in your last job?
22. What do you think of your previous boss?
23. This is a very high-pressure job; do you think you're up to it?
24. What's the most difficult challenge you've faced in your life?
25. When do you plan to retire?
26. How do you handle stress?
27. What do you do to support your professional development?
28. I'm not sure you are the right person for the job.
29. Do you think you can get along with a younger boss?
30. What kind of salary are you looking for?
31. We work a lot of late nights here; is that going to cause any trouble at home?
32. You've been out of work for a long time, haven't you?
33. What parts of your last job did you dislike?
34. Do you have commitments that would interfere with your job?
35. Have you hired or fired many

people? Give me an example of the process you used to do these tasks.

36. Why have you changed jobs so frequently?

37. You have too much experience for this job; why would you want it?

38. You've been with the same firm for so many years, how will you now cope with a new firm?

39. I'm surprised your salary isn't higher, considering everything you say you've done.

40. What was it you liked best about your last job?

41. Tell me about one of your failures at work.

42. How creative a problem solver are you?

43. How long do you expect to work for us if we offer you the job?

44. You've worked for yourself now for a while, so how will you adjust from being the boss to working for our company?

45. Give me an example of a time you had to deal with criticism from your boss.

46. Describe how you work with teams.

47. What do you do for leisure activity?

48. What qualities should a successful

manager possess?

49. Describe a large mistake you made at your last job.

50. What two accomplishments have given you the most satisfaction? Why?

51. How would you describe your ideal job?

52. How do you think your present/last boss would describe you?

53. Give me an example of how you have persuaded people to see your point of view.

54. How would you rate yourself as a leader? A supervisor? An employee?

55. What would you say are your most important accomplishments to date?

56. Describe your typical workday.

57. Describe specifically your past responsibility for managing financial budgets or department expenses.

58. Tell me about a time when your work performance was low.

59. Why do you want to change careers at your age?

60. How much of a self-starter are you?

61. If you could be in your own business, would you prefer it to corporate life?

62. How long do you think you'd be happy in this job before you started thinking about a promotion?
63. From what you understand about this job, what would you find difficult to do?
64. Describe the kinds of people you enjoy working with.
65. Tell me about a time when you observed a coworker doing something inappropriate and how you handled it.
66. Have you ever been asked to resign?
67. Were you ever fired from a job?
68. What will your spouse think about this relocation?
69. How do you deal with criticism?
70. What's the most difficult challenge you've faced in your life?
71. What are you doing now to improve yourself?
72. How many children do you have? Ages?
73. You've been unemployed for quite a while; why haven't you obtained a job before this?

Also expect technical questions on your areas of expertise. Prepare answers to any and all questions you might be asked in your specialty. Be well versed on your accomplishments, industry changes, and your thoughts on going forward, and be able to state them clearly and succinctly.

RESEARCH THE COMPANY

Review the potential company website to discover more about its goals, missions, and exactly what it does. Read its annual report, which all publicly traded companies must provide, and most make available on their website. Don't stop there. There may be more to learn.

Recently, I had a client who told me she'd found her "dream job." The organization had an admirable mission and she was thrilled to see it needed someone with her leadership skills. We checked its website and what we saw was all so positive. We created a customized resume and cover letter. Within a week she had an interview. While she was preparing for it, I told her to be sure to Google the organization to see what was being said about this nonprofit. That turned out to be a very worthwhile step. It seems that organization was involved in a lawsuit over a death, and it had been found at fault for severe negligence. Her dream job turned into a nightmare situation and she canceled the interview. Research helps you know what you are getting into. So can talking with insiders. Use your network, people from LinkedIn, your college alumni contacts, friends, etc., to get a clearer picture on what is really happening inside an organization before you meet the interviewer.

PREINTERVIEW TIPS

- Always bring your resume to the interview — don't assume that the interviewer will have it. It could have been misplaced or there could be several people at the interview.

- Bring a copy of your references and be sure phone numbers and email addresses are current and accurate. Talk to your references before you give out their names. Only include people who will say good things about you. If a former boss disliked you, use another reference who does like you.

- Work samples, excellent performance reviews, and good letters of recommendation are always impressive to an employer. Bring them.

FIRST HURDLE:
SCREENING INTERVIEW

This initial contact, which is almost always over the phone, is designed to narrow the pool of acceptable candidates, closely review qualifications, and confirm the information given on the resume in order to determine who to call in for a face-to-face interview. Expect to be thoroughly grilled during this call. The interviewer seeks to weed out the unqualified and overpriced. The caller is often an HR person; sometimes it's a recruiter; and occasionally it's your potential boss. You must pass this screening or you are out of the running.

This type of phone interview puts you at a major disadvantage since the interviewer knows he will catch you off guard. They often call in the evening or on the weekend. When you get this call, you need to be ready. Have a folder in a spot near the phone, and make sure it contains your cover letter and resume, as well as any support materials that might enhance the process.

Ask the interviewer if he can hold a moment, or if you can call him back in five minutes, so you can go to a quiet spot for this discussion. Have a pen and paper in front of you. Jot down the caller's name and take notes as he asks you questions. Smile, so your voice sounds friendly. Their job is to screen candidates and to validate applicants' backgrounds. Demonstrate that you are a great candidate with answers that offer examples of your past performance. Be concise and conversational. Sound *interested* in the job. Keep answers to less than sixty seconds to keep the interviewer focused on what you are saying. If you babble, you'll likely lose his attention and be unable to regain it.

Follow the salary negotiation techniques outlined in chapter 18 since the worst thing you can do is tell the interviewer what your salary is (or was), and he will likely ask you about it during this conversation.

Human resource professionals and recruiters mostly review your background by asking general questions. Executive recruiters are a different breed. They want to account for every moment of your professional existence. They'll spend significant time describing the job and the location if it's not in your current area in order to weed out people who likely won't move even if they get an offer. Executive recruiters also want salary information and will try to assess whether you have the background and skills to meet all the company's requirements. When you talk to an executive recruiter, ask lots of questions about the job, the duties, the position's location, travel requirements, and also about the company and its culture.

In the initial contact, you also need to use some of the time to learn as much as you can about the job, your duties, staff you may supervise, and challenges the organization is facing. It's wise to have questions written out in advance.

Be sure to add some enthusiasm into your voice. Paint a picture of how well you've performed in the past. And get a better idea of whether you want to continue pursuing this job now that you have more details.

ENGAGE THE INTERVIEWER

One CEO, who had built a $400 million company, offered this advice:

Take the time to research my company, for two reasons. First, so you can ask intelligent questions. Second, so you are prepared to talk about how your skills and background would benefit my company and give me reason to hire you. At the conclusion of the interview repeat your applicable attributes and tell me you are interested in the job. So many people I have interviewed don't do this! And it absolutely baffles me.

A decision maker and CEO reiterated something many others mentioned:

When I talk to over-40 candidates in an interview, too many focus only on telling their own story. It's all about them instead of how their experience would apply to working in my company. Basically these candidates are forgetting to focus on what they can do for me, which loses them the job.

Bottom line: prepare!

DON'T BABBLE

Nervousness can cause job candidates to talk on and on, endlessly. DMs reported this seemed to happen a great deal with the over-40 applicant. It's important to demonstrate your self-confidence and retain their interest with short, effective answers. Too often you answer a question and should just end there, but instead you keep on adding more information than necessary, which takes away from the initial answer. I once served on a hiring committee where a C-level executive took twenty minutes to answer the first question. Everyone was afraid of how bad he'd be in meetings and giving out orders once he got the job —

needless to say, he did not get hired.

Keep your answers to within a sixty-second time limit. That encourages conversation and you won't lose the interviewer by being too verbose.

KEY STRATEGY: Write out answers to questions that you might be asked in advance. Take time to think through answers so that you can clearly point out your strong points and give insightful examples demonstrating your previous work. The purpose of advance written answers is not to memorize them word for word. The purpose is to think through questions beforehand, assessing your skills, abilities, previous experience, and specific examples, and decide how to demonstrate to the employer that you can do the job. The written answers portion of the interview preparation will dramatically help you get to the real meat of your answers, and you will be better able to respond to the questions the interviewer throws at you.

Never go in cold without first practicing answering the questions out loud. Role-playing is ideal if you can get a friend or spouse to help you. This will aid you in getting smoother and more comfortable when giving your answers.

Short, concise answers that encourage conversation and an exchange of information are ideal. Whenever possible, give a specific example of how you've operated in the past. Employers want assurance that you'll be able to do the job. Offering explanations that include specific examples of how you solved a problem, saved money, contained costs, or added to the bottom line can be very influential.

TAKE NOTES —
THE EMPLOYER LIKELY WILL

For those in managerial, professional, or leadership roles, it is wise to take some notes during your interview so you can record some of the employer's more notable comments, think about a problem they have, or outline specific job duties. You may bring up an idea, a solution, or some new information that captures the company's interest. Notes help a great deal in case there are future interviews. Additionally, DMs said that note-taking really impresses the interviewer.

CLOSING THE INTERVIEW

Your interview has gone very well. You've asked all the questions that you had written down. It's time to summarize and end the interview with your 60 Second Sell. This leaves the interviewer with your most important points on what you'd bring to the position.

AFTER THE INTERVIEW

As soon as possible after the interview, sit down and note any of the tough questions you were asked and any that you feel you didn't answer well. List any questions you want to ask later if you are offered the job. Record your thoughts about the people you met, your impressions of the employer, the person interviewing you, and the company in general. Do this immediately — it can be quite valuable later. Maybe you won't get the job offer, but it's important to learn from each interview.

Send a thank-you note to anyone you interviewed with. *Emails do not count.* These are forgotten in a moment, so be sure you handwrite a personal note. Mail it the same day if possible. If you ask the interviewer for his or her business card, you'll have the correct name and address. In your note, reiterate one or two of the benefits that you'd bring to the organization and state your interest in the job. Many DMs said that a thank-you note is influential especially if the employer is wavering between two people.

SUMMARY

Research the company, the job, and the potential boss to get as much information as you can about the needs of the organization. As you prepare for each interview, be very clear about the employer's needs. Stress the strengths, abilities, skills, and past experiences that you're bringing to the employer's job. Prepare a 5-Point Agenda and a 60 Second Sell. Write out answers to questions in advance, and then practice verbally, answering questions either in a mock interview or on a tape recorder. Edit answers to improve them. Throughout the interview, give specific examples that describe the work you've done in the past. Compile questions that you plan to ask the interviewer. Be sure to dodge questions on salary until after you have been offered the job. Prior to any interview, do read chapter 16 on how to wow employers with your personal presentation, and you will feel more confident knowing you are doing the very best you can to ace the interview.

CHAPTER 18
SALARY NEGOTIATIONS

"Effort equals results."

ROBIN RYAN

Congratulations! You got the job offer. Some hard negotiations can take place in this final stage. If you've been following the guidelines set forth in this book, you haven't shared with the employer your salary desires or benefits, so he or she is not sure where you stand on these issues.

Before you go into negotiations you need to be prepared. Keep this fact in mind: *the largest salary increases you'll likely ever earn are when you go to work for a new employer.*

Extensive employment compensation studies support this fact. In fact, most of my clients whom I help in salary negotiation end up getting a better compensation package than they originally wanted or were offered. So you have a lot at stake. Whether you are employed or unemployed, whether you are looking for a $500,000 base or a $60,000 one, you must become skilled in the process of salary negotiation. And there are a lot of perks and bonus structures to discuss too. You have already overcome the biggest hurdle — you have demonstrated your value to the employer and gotten the job offer.

The tide has now turned. The employer is no longer screening you — they know they want you, and they are recruiting you to take the position. It's a great spot to be sitting in. You have demonstrated your value and now have an excellent opportunity to negotiate a higher salary or increased benefits.

WHO EARNS WHAT?

A little background is necessary to give you some perspective. According to the U.S. government salary reports, here are some facts about what Americans actually earn:

- The over-40 worker's average salary is $80,000.
- They have 3.5 weeks of vacation.
- In large companies with more than 100,000 employees worldwide, the average salary when you are over 40 is $100,000.

- MBAs earn the highest salaries.
- People with a bachelor's degree earn almost $24,000 more annually than those with some college education but no bachelor's.
- Doctorates earn $97,000 on average.
- People with a professional degree (MDs, dentists, lawyers) earn $100,000 and up.
- 7% of individuals over 40 earn over $100,000.
- Less than 1% earn over $500,000.
- Men earn 23% higher salaries than women.

Of course salaries vary by job title, field, and location. Many of you make well over $100,000; some much less. But if you are over 40, you are in your peak earning years, and you certainly want to maximize the dollars an employer pays you.

Preserving their salary is of key importance to many of my clients. They don't want to "start over" and take a big salary cut, and neither do you. If you have been applying for "good fit" jobs, and you have a strong resume and cover letter that outline your value to the decision makers, your interview must have been strong, too, because now they have offered you the job.

The next few interactions with the employer can put thousands of more dollars into your paycheck — or, if you are like many women and you *don't* ask, you'll leave a lot of money on the table that the company was willing to pay you to join the team. Therefore women and men must both try to negotiate. The guidelines explaining how to do that best follow.

GET THE JOB OFFER FIRST

In my audio program *Salary Negotiation Strategies* (WWW.ROBINRYAN.COM/STORE), I reveal the cardinal rule of this process:

> Don't reveal your previous salary — ever!

Wait to discuss money and benefits until after the company has made you an offer. Only then do you have the most power to suggest they offer more in salary, vacation days, and other perks — and *get them!* I've had clients who came to see me after they learned a very hard lesson. They had *lost out* on jobs because early in the interview they told the hiring manager or recruiter their actual salary. One HR recruiter, who was a friend of the client, actually clued her in that once the hiring manager heard the

338

low figure that the current employer paid her, he devalued her skills as "low level." Too late, she learned the correct salary negotiation technique is to never reveal a previous salary. She never made that mistake again. A few weeks later, she masterfully dodged the salary questions when interviewing with an impressive high-tech company. Coupled with good answers and solid work examples, she *doubled* the pay of the job she left, landing a great midlevel management position. If you are asked in an interview, "What salary do you currently make?" simply volley the question back with one of your own. Reply with "What is the salary range that this job pays?"

DON'T SEND SALARY HISTORY

Employer requests for a salary history when applying for a job should just be ignored. But if the ad insists, stating, "We won't consider anyone who doesn't send a salary history," you can comply in a clever way that preserves your negotiating power. Instead of revealing your old salary, offer a statement of fact, citing a salary survey source. (These are available from professional associations, in business magazines, or on my website, where you'll find salary calculators, learn about relocation costs, and find cost-of-living tools — go to WWW.ROBINRYAN.COM/BOOKREADER.)

Do your homework. You should have already reviewed what your years of experience and skills are worth in the marketplace. When I ask seminar participants or clients that question, most don't have an answer. So your first task is to find out.

Decision makers report that they use the salary question as a device to *screen out applicants.* While you worry the employer won't pay high enough, in reality oftentimes employers eliminate you because your salary is too low, thus automatically downgrading their perception of your skills. One client came for help after she'd lost a new job opportunity by bringing in her W-2 form. She was proud to show the potential employer that she'd made $136,000 the year before, but that cost her the job since the starting salary for the new position began at over $200,000. Be sure to do your research so you are aware of what the salary is and that you are within the true range of the position.

Be careful of another clever trick potential employers use, and always leave the salary boxes blank on job applications. This is a legal document and if you "fudge" on the true number, background checks often reveal your true salary, which can result in your being fired after they hire you. When asked about salaries you made at previous jobs on electronic applications, try leaving those boxes blank; if that doesn't work try typing in "salary bonus" or using "open." If none of that allows your application process to go through, try typing in "0," which is obviously a mistake since you won't work for nothing.

KNOW WHAT YOU WANT

Again, do your homework. List the perks you previously received and decide which ones are most important to you. Consider:

- Salary level
- Bonus structure and percentage
- Vacation length
- Medical — Was it fully paid? Partially paid? Cost for you? Cost to add your family? Does it have a large deductible?
- Stock options — get the details and specifics on vesting, buying, and selling
- Use of a car
- Laptop/phone/BlackBerry
- Paid parking
- Day care

- Retirement plan and company contribution
- Training opportunities
- Relocation or separation packages

Write out anything else you may have received that matters to you.

Many of you could get a signing bonus simply by asking for one. These are typical, but not always brought up in the initial offer, so *be sure you ask for a signing bonus.*

Relocation benefits are getting trickier because houses are harder to sell and companies are refusing to buy them. Do your best to get as large a relocation package as you can. These have been the deal breakers recently since many executives are underwater on their house's equity or the family flat-out refuses to move. If you know this is a major problem for you, consider it more in depth before you apply for a job halfway across the country. Renting out their existing home is one solution many clients have taken to move to a new job in another state.

You should have already reviewed what your years of experience and skills are worth in the marketplace. When I ask seminar participants or clients that question most don't have an answer. So your first task is to find out.

Next, know your bottom line — what is the lowest salary you will accept. Be ready to walk — there are other employers out there and you may need to wait a bit longer to find a better-paying position.

SUBSTANTIATING YOUR VALUE TO THE ORGANIZATION

Let's look at how my client Mark handled his negotiations. He was a corporate manager making $120,000 before he was laid off. Money follows value, so my first step with this client was to help him see that the employer who was offering him a new job needed his skill set and would care very little, if at all, that Mark was unemployed. But the DM would more likely start at the lower end of what he or she was willing to pay just to see if Mark would take it. Mark had learned that when you're negotiating for a higher salary than what is offered, you're going to have to defend your value position. You must make it clear to the employer *why* you're worth the extra money. List the benefits that hiring you brings the employer. Point out any aspects of your experience that the employer has already praised to reiterate what experience the company gets if you join the team. What are

343

your strengths and experiences that will assist your new manager in doing the job? Point out exactly why you deserve the extra income you're requesting. Point out that your training and experience will result in less "learning time." Most companies realize it takes people anywhere from three to six months to learn a new job, and there's a relatively slow and unproductive period at the beginning. Demonstrate how you can hit the ground running and/or be highly productive very quickly. You may also want to mention something he or she doesn't know yet and show how the company gets extra value. Make connections between your skills and the skills that the job requires. Would you actually walk away from the position? Sure you would if the deal isn't good enough, but *never bluff* as a negotiation tactic — it may cost you the job.

WHAT TO SAY WHEN YOU WANT TO GET MORE $$$ AND PERKS

Mark's initial offer was $112,000 and he thought that was really the bottom of the scale for his type of position. Mark began the negotiation (just as you will) by saying, "I was disappointed in your offer since I have such value I can bring to your team. I thought it was a bit too low." Mark offered the DM three solid reasons why he was perfect for the job. The DM said, "Oh? What would be more in line with your expectations to join our team?" Mark replied, "Well, I was expecting something in the upper $120s or low $130s." The DM responded by saying, "Well, that is higher than we planned for this position." Mark waited. The DM thought about it for maybe one whole minute and said, "Let's agree on a figure before I go to my boss and HR and see if we can come to an agreement." Mark was up-front and said, "I'd be happy to accept the job with a base salary of $128,000, assuming the package of perks is similar to what I've had before." Mark was willing to come down if necessary but he did not let the DM know that. They discussed the other benefits, including an extra week's vacation and a signing bonus of $5,000.

Competition sometimes influences an employer to think about your request. If she decides the other prospects aren't quite up to snuff, she may offer significantly more money. Conversely, she may be willing to go to the number two choice if you are too expensive. You must sincerely believe in yourself and know that you can make a good contribution to this employer. At this point, tell the DM that you believe you can make a solid contribution, but that you expect to be fairly compensated. Use those words: "fairly compensated."

Another aspect of salary negotiation is to explore market surveys on the typical salary for the job you are being offered. You could say, "In several of the companies I've been talking to, I have found that the salary for this type of position is normally between $105,000 and $139,000." You can even mention one or two competitors to make the employer aware that you have other opportunities and that you know what the market pays for the types of services you are offering. Be sure your market figures are accurate — cite your sources.

In Mark's case, the DM came back with a salary increase and agreed to give Mark the job with an extra week off. But he said they weren't doing hiring bonuses right now. Instead he offered to vest him with some company stock for his retirement plan after six months, and Mark and the interviewer had a deal.

Most employers have some flexibility in negotiating salary. They're not trying to exploit job applicants, but they also don't want to pay more than necessary. If you're willing to accept less, they might as well pay you less. Salaries are usually assigned to the job, not to the individual, but people performing the same job are not equal in terms of productivity and results. Since individual performance differs, you should establish your value in the eyes of the employer rather than target a salary figure for the job. When you have clearly defined your value to yourself, you can convey it to the employer and usually emerge as a winner in the negotiations battle.

NEGOTIATING AN EXIT SEVERANCE PACKAGE ON THE WAY IN

Vice presidents, C-level people, and those in other high-level positions are beginning to write in clauses to ensure greater stability in their jobs. Some want a contract for a specified service length of time — say three years — with an automatic renewal. Some employers agree to these terms. This is frequently the case with high-level nonprofit and academic positions.

Corporations aren't crazy about these binding terms. Of course employers want to have loopholes to fire you at will, and you want some protection. And if you have relocated, you don't want to be stuck repaying thousands of dollars back to the company. Forget trying to get something about "firing only for cause" in your hiring letter.

Believe me, they'll make up a cause if they want you out. Many CEOs I've worked with have learned that the hard way. I advise my high-level clients to add a predetermined severance clause to their hiring letter. This clause covers both mergers and terminations. It may be wise to check with your own lawyer to outline your demands if you decide to add a severance/termination clause.

For example, your employment letter might state something like this:

[Employer name] can fire this employee, [your name], at any time for any reason, as long as one of the two following conditions are met.

1. Employer must grant this employee, [your name], 18 months' notice, maintaining employee's current pay levels for 18 months.

OR

2. For immediate departure of [your name] the [company name] agrees to pay [your name] a one-year (12 months) lump sum salary payment on day of departure. Additionally, the employer agrees to pay for ongoing medical insurance benefits through the company's policy for one year, or until

employee gets a new position, which-
ever comes first.

If you have a complex deal — and some
of you do — with relocation paybacks, non-
competing clauses, etc., and for anyone adding in a severance clause I recommend that
you consult a lawyer to protect yourself and
your interests.

Once the negotiations are complete, make
your decision. It is permissible to take a day
or two to consider all aspects. You may wish
to consult another company where you've
also been interviewing to determine their
status and if you are still being considered.
It's best to learn exactly what your options
are and not guess.

You may discover in the negotiation interview that everything isn't as rosy as the
employer painted it when he initially interviewed you. Be sure you have an accurate
picture of the job and the workplace culture
before you accept. You don't want big sur-
prises once you get there, like learning that
you have a large budget deficit to handle, or
that two problem employees have run off
two managers in the last year. Sometimes,
through negotiation, you learn a lot about
the real workplace you'll be joining, and if
it varies from how it was presented in the

interview process.

GET IT IN WRITING

Once you've finished negotiating salary, and you and the employer have decided on an acceptable amount, reconfirm everything about the job. Employers often have short memories and might exaggerate how good business is, or the extra perks may not be exactly the way they were explained in the negotiation process. If the DM said the company has flextime, but it was vague in the employee manual, ask coworkers about the actual practice. Same with comp time — can you really use it or is that discouraged and frowned on by managers? Restate all the terms, and then get it in writing. Request an *employment offer letter* — this is essential to your future. *Do not say "contract"; say "letter."* A job offer letter is very common and doesn't require a lawyer to create it. A letter of intent to hire should state the title, the salary, start date, a brief job description, and any special arrangements or benefits that you've agreed to. This doesn't have to be a legal masterpiece, but it could be important for future reference. Many job hunters tell horror stories of having negotiated something verbally, only to discover it doesn't happen after they start the job. Apparently, a DM can have "selective memory" on that promised extra week off, so a letter can be important insurance for both parties.

SUMMARY

The key to your negotiations is to be prepared and try to negotiate as good a deal as possible. You get these chances only a few times in your career so go after as much as that employer is willing to pay. Maybe this isn't the job for you after all. Waiting may pay off.

Look at company benefits and analyze their cost or savings to you. Ask about the cost of medical benefits for you and your family. Many companies pay medical benefits only for the employee; family members are covered by an employee deduction. If insuring your family will cost $300 per month that's $3,600 a year after taxes. Perhaps at your current job, medical benefits are completely covered. Use that bargaining chip and say, "In my current position I have full medical coverage, and this out-of-pocket cost to insure my family here is $3,600. I really need to get that included in the salary to make your offer more attractive." Human resource managers are often willing to make adjustments on this issue. Even though benefit costs keep rising, you will have negotiated extra salary to cover them.

There are several other issues you can negotiate, including extra vacation, an expense account, a car, etc. Clarify overtime and how or if it is paid. Ask for a copy of the employee handbook; it outlines policies and procedures on vacation and personal leave. All these factors can aid you in making your decision.

THE FINAL DECISION

No one can put a price tag on job satisfaction. Liking your job should be one of your top objectives. Other factors, such as potential career growth and promotional opportunities, often enter into the picture, but your personal satisfaction and the reward that comes from a job you enjoy is priceless. A close look at the corporate culture before embarking on a career change will help prevent you from accepting the wrong job.

■ ■ ■ ■

Part 5
LIVING A
BETTER
FUTURE

■ ■ ■ ■

"It takes no more effort to expect the best than to fear the worst."

ROBIN RYAN

CHAPTER 19
SET S.M.A.R.T. GOALS

"Action turns your dreams into reality."
ROBIN RYAN

Behavioral psychologists claim that by setting written goals, you can achieve your desired accomplishments 20% faster. Yet research reveals that less than 3% of Americans write down their goals, and less than 1% rewrite and review their goals on a daily basis. Goal setting is a powerful tool that can make a significant difference in your job search success. You must have a burning desire to achieve your goal and single-mindedly focus on it until it becomes a reality. If you are not serious and committed, you probably won't get where you want to be.

Why bother with this action step? Most high achievers say the key to their success was setting highly defined goals. Successful people continue to set goals to push themselves on to higher levels of achievement. If you set as your goal a job that will produce personal satisfaction and appropriate financial rewards to support your desired lifestyle, you will be motivated to fulfill your own potential and make your goal a reality.

Goal setting doesn't come naturally. Most of us were raised in families that did not expect or expose us to personal goal setting. Many professional athletes credit their fathers who set goals for them as small children and both parents who encouraged them to continue to set new goals. For others, coaches encouraged goal setting: a faster time, a higher jump, stretching and reaching until they achieved the next level of athletic achievement.

Only you can set goals for your job hunt. Only you can take the action steps to research and call employers, set up meetings, present your skills and abilities, write a terrific resume, craft engaging cover letters, and develop a 60 Second Sell along with good interview answers. These proactive steps take time, energy, and commitment. It's in following the process and advice laid out in this book that you can realize your dreams and get the job you really want.

Many people fear rejection and failure, yet that is an intrinsic part of job hunting. No one can guarantee that you'll be able to find a new job quickly and easily. (In fact, it usually takes anywhere from four to ten months.) Don't expect that you'll encounter positive people all along the way and receive multiple job offers. There will be exciting highs, but you can be sure there also will be devastating rejections. You will undoubtedly meet some employers whose needs you don't exactly fit. Some opportunities will pass you by. You may apply for a lot of openings but never receive a response. Try to look at these not as failures but as efforts that are a prerequisite for success.

If you don't fail and get a little rejection along the way, are you really trying? And if you're not trying, you'll never succeed.

Stay focused on the new career position you want. Visualize how it will change your life, how it will positively affect your lifestyle, and the rewards it will bring in money and personal satisfaction. Goal setting will inspire your energy and actions.

ROBIN'S S.M.A.R.T. GOAL-SETTING PROCESS

Goals are a precise statement of your vision, and setting goals means noting all the endeavors that you must undertake if you are to achieve the desired outcome. Use clear statements of the specific action steps required to achieve the goals, starting from today. Remember, behavioral psychologists say that *positive outcomes are typically achieved 20% faster with written goals.*

S.M.A.R.T. Goals is a savvy but simple tool for goal setting that specifically identifies your desired outcome, details an action plan, and facilitates accomplishment.

Here is the formula:

- **SPECIFIC** — Write out a clearly defined goal and a list of the action steps necessary to reach it.
- **MEASURABLE** — You and others must be readily able to see how you are progressing, every step of the way.
- **ACHIEVABLE** — Your goal may be a stretch from where you are now, but it is certainly doable.
- **REALISTIC** — Set sensible goals and objectives that you can expect to achieve by relying on your own efforts.
- **TARGETED** — Know exactly where you are going and how you are going to get there, and define the consequences and potential rewards to anticipate realizing the goal.

Each morning before you do anything else,

review your goals. Repeat these to yourself — better yet, state them out loud. (The shower is a great place for this little exercise.)

Focus on what you want and precisely where you want to be when your job search is over. Define what you're looking for. Invest private time at the outset of your job hunt to do whatever soul-searching and internal investigating is necessary to create a targeted self-marketing plan. In the long run, this approach will be the most effective way to get a good job.

ROADBLOCKS: FEELINGS AND ATTITUDES

Job hunting is full of tough choices and compromises. You might have been sought after and recruited to your current job, but the rules have changed for those over 40. Today, job hunters are forced to take a proactive, "I'm going to do whatever it takes!" stance. You want to succeed. From years of working with job hunters, let me offer some thoughts to make your job search easier.

Feelings such as fear, rejection, and desperation can present major roadblocks. A client once told me, "I was fired. No one will want me now!" He projected the image of a loser: no self-confidence, no attempt to try new techniques. But over time, he changed his attitude, focused on his strengths and the type of work situation that best showcased them, and networked. He got a great job!

Another seminar participant came up to me and said, "I can't call strangers. I won't do it." And she didn't. Her timid, fearful attitude left her unemployed for twelve months.

The wife of a man who had gotten fired called with deep concern. "My husband lost his job over a month ago, and he's so embarrassed he won't tell anyone." He's in shock — but a pity party can't last more than a few days. You must get help if you are that down and depressed. Hiding in your house, like this man was doing, will not get you hired.

Fear is real: fear of rejection, fear of failure, and fear of the unknown will stop your forward progress faster than anything else. Fear goes hand in hand with depression. Together, they lead to desperation. Panic and desperation must be dealt with and controlled. Otherwise you won't project self-confidence, which is essential to success.

The job search process includes rejection. You'll win some and you'll lose a lot more.

But you will succeed in the end if you keep following the plan we've laid out for you in this book. If you feel like you need more help, go to my website, WWW.ROBINRYAN .COM. There are a lot of tools there. I do offer individual career counseling, resume writing, and interview coaching — so don't feel desperate — you are *not* alone. Help is available if you need an expert to assist you.

TIME MANAGEMENT AND YOUR ACTION PLAN

No career counselor can wave a magic wand and get you a new position whenever you want one. But using good time management and a job search action plan will make your searching easier.

Expect to spend months on an active job search. If you are not presently employed, devote twenty-five hours a week to your job hunt. Include structured activities in your weekly action plan. Spend each week networking and responding to leads and openings by producing targeted resumes and cover letters. Set up appointments, research the job market, and look for new job leads. Schedule informational interviews, ask and get more referral sources, and set up more meetings and phone conversations. Your days will be full. In your off time do something where you can see an end result. Paint your garage. Work out and lose weight. Clean out your closets. Have a garage sale and get rid of stuff you don't want, or sell it on eBay. Take on an activity you enjoy: gardening, playing golf, scrapbooking, playing with kids or grandkids. You need some fun in your life to keep your spirits positive since this is a long process. Your attitude — positive, focused, and committed to your success — is the key.

If you have a full-time job, you may have to limit the number of hours per week that you can devote to your job search. About four to seven hours is a realistic goal if you are already working forty-plus hours a week. Then cherry-pick! Apply only for positions you really want or are well qualified to hold. You don't have time to pursue every position you run across, so be very selective.

Squeeze in phone calls during the lunch hour, do some online research, check job boards, and also schedule time to write cover letters. Work on your resume. Meet with contacts. Have a priority system. Don't waste your precious free time with something that is not worthwhile. Use your evenings, early mornings, and lunch times. Plan each week's activities carefully to keep you on track toward your job search goal.

A job search action plan form is available as a free download to you as an added bonus for buying this book. It contains charts, forms, and a record-keeping section all ready for you to use.

Go to WWW.ROBINRYAN.COM/BOOKREADER to get yours.

LISTENING TO YOUR DREAMS

What you say to yourself has more influence and more effect on your job search than you will ever realize. Don't allow yourself to dwell on negative thoughts. Avoid phrases such as:

- "I've tried everything and there are no jobs out there."
- "No one's hiring a person who's over 40 years old [or 45, 50, 56, 62]."
- "They don't want me."
- "The economy is terrible. I may as well just stay at the job I have and accept that I'm lucky to *have* a job."
- "No one needs someone with my skills."

Negativity leads to depression and desperation, which will be transmitted to potential employers, damaging your chances. On the other hand, a positive mental state allows you to radiate confidence.

Look into books and audiotapes that teach positive self-talk. If you aren't sure what to select, try my audio series called the *Ultimate You Success Series,* at WWW.ROBINRYAN .COM/STORE. What you believe and think shapes your attitude. Tell yourself, "I have great skills and an employer is going to be excited about hiring me because of all the contributions I can make to her company." Positive thoughts such as these can help to change your emotional state and trigger actions that reflect self-confidence and enthusiasm to an employer. These affirmations are positive thoughts or ideas and they do help. Repeat them daily.

When one opportunity falls through, you will feel the sting of rejection. Keep in mind that you still have a long list of potential employers to fall back on. Expand your horizons. Perhaps you have set too narrow a target: going after only one employer, or restricting yourself to a certain commute, special work hours, or a specific location. Consider being more flexible and more open to seeing opportunities you might have overlooked. Examine your transferable skills and explore new fields to expand the scope of your job search.

CHAPTER 20
YOU'RE HIRED!

"You are the architect of your life, and
only you can plan it, improve it,
and make it more fulfilling."

ROBIN RYAN

I spend my days working with real people
just like you, advising them on how to use
these techniques to land a terrific job. I also
spend a lot of time talking to HR managers,
and anyone who hires and makes the decisions concerning who gets the job and who
doesn't. I do this so I can offer my clients,
and you, the best information and strategy
possible. I continually learn and in fact
learned some new things researching this
book that are already benefiting my current
clients in achieving their success.

Your goals, needs, and hopes are different
now from what they were ten years ago.
Change can be good for all of us; it allows
us to grow and reengage. We all need to

revitalize our career from time to time. My goal for you is that you find a new job that makes you feel better about who you are, and about what you contribute to others and the organization you work for. As we age, getting fulfillment from our work takes on a larger meaning for us. You may want a higher-level job and are willing to work hard to get it. Many of you want to maintain your success, but prefer to work less and not as hard as you did to get there. Some have empty households and want to do more traveling. Still others seek to eliminate the travel from their jobs. Many still want a challenge to keep work interesting. And most need to continue earning money.

Some folks are done with a major career. You may be looking for part-time work or just more time off. You may want to walk away from the past (well, let's say build on it a bit) and do something completely different.

What is certain is that you want a job — and not just any job but one that matters and will fit with your current goals, personal desires, and needs. The quickest way to become successful is to find out what you do best, and then excel in it.

A heavy dose of self-belief is critical. Reading this book and following the advice it presents on resume writing, job hunting techniques, and interviewing are important, but so is your dedication to driving yourself to achieve success. Don't rely on luck or things outside your control as part of your success plan.

Since you want to be successful in your career endeavors, let's review what it takes to achieve big goals. Successful people think differently. They take 100% responsibility for their lives. Successful men and women find out what it's going to cost to make their next career dream come true. Then they find a way to make it happen. Most importantly, they don't complain about the work it takes to achieve their dreams. You can get practically anything you want in life — if you are willing to pay the price. You must *focus,* which requires giving up some things in the present. You realize the time invested will pay off big-time down the road. Every week, ask yourself, "Is what I'm doing right now bringing me closer to my career goal?" If it's not, do something that will.

Taking the time to write an action plan, to map out how you're going to achieve your goals, is one of the best ways to get where you're going, faster. Without a mapped-out plan, you'll experience frustration and waste time and energy. With a map in hand, you're virtually assured of arriving at your destination in the shortest time possible.

No one ever said that reaching your goals and obtaining success was easy. If you truly desire to achieve success in life, you must be willing to overcome obstacles on the way to reaching your goals and dreams. Approach your goals and dreams with a positive attitude. Having a negative attitude and thinking that you can't accomplish your goals and be successful in life will only slow you down. Stay positive even if the road gets tough, and you'll be that much closer to achieving success. When you're truly committed to achieving your goal, giving up isn't even an option. You are willing to do whatever it takes to make it happen. And so it does!

Do It Now!

Every one of us takes life for granted. That is, until fate, or we ourselves, intervene.

Many of us live in the comfortable illusion that our life will go on forever. We squander so many days of our precious existence. We fail to recognize how vulnerable we are until the unexpected happens. Then, we tend to step back and assess who we are, what we've done, what truly matters, and what we'd still like to accomplish. The past is history and cannot be changed. The future is pure fantasy. *Now* is all that matters.

Your life is made up of choices. You control the job you have, the amount of success that you experience, where you live, who your friends are, and what you do.

Let me assure you that right now *is* the time to take a long, hard look at what's most important to you. Decide what it is that will make you truly happy. Relish being you! Be the best person possible. You are unique and special. Let the world know it.

THEY DID IT AND SO CAN YOU

Many of my clients have used the strategies outlined in this book, and they all have had the same conclusion — the strategies really work. And they landed new jobs — good ones. Great ones — dream jobs they never thought they'd ever find, let alone acquire. That's why I'm convinced following the process in this book will work for you.

Many of the over-40 people I encounter fit into one of these situations:

- They have been laid off or fear they will be.
- They dislike their current job and want another.

- They are striving to move ahead and seek a promotion.
- They have a multiyear employment gap and are now interested in returning to work.
- They want to change careers, to find a more satisfying situation.

Here are some examples of real people from my client files. What they faced, and how they succeeded in their job search, should help inspire you.

JEFF — a highly paid senior executive who got fired

JULIA — a laid-off marketing director who wouldn't consider relocation

LISA — a newly divorced mom returning to work

PATRICIA — wanted the top job

STEVE — wanted a promotion, but lacked a degree

ALAN — hated his job and wanted a fresh start

JANICE — wanted a new career in a different field

All of these clients were over-40 candidates; each person faced serious obstacles in re-creating themselves. But all were able to transform themselves, learn how to self-market their strengths, and update their personal image to become highly desirable candidates.

Jeff was a 56-year-old talented chief of operations who had been highly paid and well liked. A new CEO took over, and the next fourteen months became a nightmare for Jeff. He clashed with his CEO on just about everything and was finally fired. He'd been a fine employee, moving up through the ranks over the past fifteen years. When we first met, he was quite depressed, and he needed to completely update his appearance — his suit didn't fit, his hairstyle was old-fashioned, and his shoulders slumped. He seemed worn out — far removed from the image of the vibrant executive he needed to portray. A new resume, well-defined answers to questions about his firing, a contemporary suit, and a new hairstyle transformed him. He got several interviews at interesting companies and accepted a new exciting job as a CEO. The company offered Jeff a terrific relocation package and a salary increase of $75,000, making it significantly higher than his previous salary. For a man who came to me worried that no one would ever hire him again, he did very well.

Julia was a working mother in her early

50s with shared custody of teenagers when she got laid off. She was a VP of sales in an industry that was disappearing. She couldn't relocate, so looking into a new field was her only option. She became a client because she needed a new resume. She told me it was pitiful and she wasn't exaggerating. Selling a product was easy for her; selling herself and her talents was not. There weren't too many opportunities available where she lived. She turned down one offer because the salary was $85,000 and she had been making $135,000 as her base salary. A friend introduced her to the president of a company at a social gathering. They talked briefly then she later called to follow up. He scheduled her for an interview, and she really did her homework. She'd researched this interesting new field until she could talk about it intelligently, and she sold her relationship-building skills. It worked! The offer came in at $125,000, plus a commission. After her first year she emailed me to say she'd made about $160,000. She's still employed with the same company, having found the new field interesting and financially rewarding.

Lisa married at age 20. She had some secretarial skills but little else before she started a family. She was in her early 40s when her marriage ended. She had no education beyond high school so her prospects were limited. She also had children so she needed flexibility in her position. She had some artistic talent and thought about doing promotions but couldn't find a position that paid a decent wage. We reviewed her interests and discovered that one thing she loved was makeup. In fact, during prom season, several girls gathered at her house so she could "make them look beautiful." She embraced this hobby and started talking to managers at a mall department store.

One cosmetic product line was seeking a department manager, and Lisa sold talents she'd gotten from some volunteer work and landed the job. It was a great fit, and it has proved to be a terrific way for her to get back to work and earn a decent salary with the much-needed benefits.

Patricia had been a CFO for a health-care company for seven years and done a lot to add to growing revenues. When it was announced that the CEO was retiring she decide to go after that job. The promotion was one she felt she was qualified for. The only problem was, the departing CEO didn't think so, and he said he would not support her candidacy to the board of directors. She and I worked hard on preparing for her interview. We met a couple of times to strategize and develop her interview skills. She went to the interview feeling as if she could climb Mount Everest. Her confidence impressed the board of directors, and she is now their CEO.

Steve had been a store merchandise buyer who wanted a promotion into corporate retail management. When he was 49, his company went under and he was forced to look for new employment. His biggest obstacle was that he lacked a college degree. He'd also been with this same company his whole career. Once he created a good resume, he secured a few interviews with other chains, but his lack of a college degree stopped him from moving beyond the first inquiry from HR. Since going to college for three years to finish a bachelor's degree seemed out of the question, he refocused his search. He needed to expand his search, network at levels above HR, and update his approach to show that he was open-minded and could adapt to a new company. He had a strong resume focused on buying, but not much management experience. We worked on strategy and interviewing to show his strengths and the benefits he could bring to an organization. He found a position that caught his eye. It combined both purchasing and sales. He succeeded in landing this job and advancing his career into corporate management. He also secured a starting salary of $77,000 and a great 30% bonus structure.

Alan was a very smart lawyer holding a general counsel position. He was highly paid, making over $250,000 annually. Few people earn as much money as he did, but Alan had grown to absolutely hate his job. In his early 50s, with a family to support, he wanted to move out of the current firm, but salary was a very big consideration. He realized relocation was a necessity if he wanted to continue to earn a high salary — and one of his primary objectives was to go into a position where he felt the company's mission was important. His five-page resume had gotten him no interviews, and we rewrote it. The new resume helped potential employers to see his talent. He looked for positions as general counsel and found a few that looked promising. With a good, solid resume ready, we worked on his interviewing skills. He actually flew to Seattle to do his interview practice session with me in person. He was offered two jobs in one week and accepted one in Dallas, grateful to be able to move into a much better situation than he left. The salary was

$35,000 more, and the cost of living was less, so it proved to be a profitable transition.

Janice wanted a new career. She'd retired from teaching at age 57, leaving the $52,000 job she'd worked at for over thirty years. Within two years, though, her 401(k) retirement account got hurt in the stock market crash, leading her to consider working again. She told me she was finished with teaching and wanted to do something completely different. She also had a new grandbaby and wanted only a part-time job. Finding work at age 59 made her feel a little like a dinosaur. No one would hire her. Even when she got an interview, she said she could see the hiring manager's face drop when she showed up "looking old." She asked, "What can you do for me?" I taught her about the hidden job market and helped her to see she had transferable skills. But to make her more marketable in her new career choice, she needed to go back to school to get some computer skills. After she got that training, it allowed her to get hired at a great hourly wage, working only three days a week. That turned out to be exactly what she had dreamed about.

SUMMARY

These people were all over 40 and needed to learn a new way to job hunt. Many found the details on using the hidden job market very useful. It improved their search efforts and had a significant, positive impact on their results — they got new jobs.

They had to re-create themselves with a relevant resume, engaging cover letter, better interviewing skills, and a new, more contemporary, look. They did that, too. I've worked with a great many career counseling clients who pushed on to find success. When they met decision makers or HR people, all were ready to show the employer they still had a lot to offer.

Developing an effective self-marketing approach was essential to these people landing a new or better job. They made changes, just as you need to do. These clients tried new things to lead them through the months it took to reach their goal. They did not give up. I am sure several got discouraged and some were depressed and frustrated that the job search process is so long and tough and lacks any immediate gratification. Job hunting is not easy — it is hard work!

Following the job search program outlined in this book yields end results that are worth it. You'll land a new job — one that makes you happy. I've seen a lot of people over 40, over 50, and over 60 move on to find something that turned out to be a great fit for each of them.

Each person must find his or her own road to success, but hopefully now you have a blueprint for what works. Once you have mastered the techniques and implemented the needed changes and new strategies we've discussed in this book, you never need feel helpless again. No threat of unemployment will terrify you. You'll be ahead of the game, managing your own career and knowing you can direct it to get exactly what you want.

I know that you will find the same success my clients have, and that your new job and a prosperous future are just ahead.

CAREER RESOURCES
TO HELP YOU

CAREER COUNSELING
AND JOB SEARCH SERVICES

Robin Ryan offers telephone consulting and in-person services to clients from all fifty states and Canada, with programs to meet your budget:

- Resume creation
- Cover letters
- Interview coaching
- Job search guidance
- Salary negotiations
- Career guidance
- Changing careers
- Reentering the workforce
- Career advancement

Robin can help you succeed with an ultimate job search program, guiding you from start to finish.

Contact Robin at 425.226.0414
Email her at robin@robinryan.com
Visit her website at: WWW.ROBINRYAN
.COM

AVAILABLE BOOKS, AUDIO TRAINING, AND MP3 DOWNLOADS

The *San Francisco Chronicle* referred to Robin Ryan's "Ultimate Job Search Toolbox" as the "most effective job search resource ever assembled."

This job search package contains all her bestselling books and audio programs.

Robin Ryan has authored other popular books, including:

- *60 Seconds & You're Hired!*
- *Winning Resumes*, 2nd Edition
- *Winning Cover Letters*, 2nd Edition
- *What to Do with the Rest of Your Life*
- *Soaring on Your Strengths*

Her popular audio CDs and MP3 downloads include:

- *The Ultimate You Audio Success Series*
- *Salary Negotiation Strategies*
- *The Career Change Workbook* and audio CD series
- *Networking Strategies for Career Success*

- *60 Seconds & You're Hired!*
- *Over 40 & You're Hired!*

All are available at her website store: WWW
.ROBINRYAN.COM

ROBIN RYAN IS AVAILABLE TO SPEAK TO YOUR GROUP

- Keynote addresses
- Seminars
- Workshops
- Retreats
- Telecasts
- Webinars
- Full-/half-day training programs

Contact Robin Ryan today to discuss your program needs at 425.226.0414
Email: speakingevents@robinryan.com

FREE DOWNLOADS, TOOLS, EXTRA CONTENT EXCLUSIVE TO BOOK BUYERS

Job hunting? Here's some extra help — and it's free only to book buyers of *Over 40 & You're Hired!*

Throughout the pages in this book, Robin has listed a unique website URL address to give you free resources that are restricted to book buyers only.

You can download *free* files and PDFs,

including:

- Job search tools
- Current recommended job listing web-sites
- Salary tools to determine your true value in today's workplace
- Cost-of-living and relocation resources
- Photos of impressive interview attire with makeovers for men and women
- Charts
- Templates
- Job search action plan
- Quizzes
- Plus more guidance and content

Look for the special website page address listed throughout this book.

FREE NEWSLETTER

Learn more about Robin Ryan and how to manage your career more effectively with her advice and articles. Sign up for her free newsletter at WWW.ROBINRYAN.COM.

ABOUT THE AUTHOR

Oprah, Dr. Phil, NBC Nightly News, Fox News, and CNN are only a few of the more than one thousand TV and radio shows where **Robin Ryan** has been seen offering her advice.

She is the best-selling author of *60 Seconds & You're Hired!, Soaring on Your Strengths, Winning Resumes, Winning Cover Letters,* and *What to Do with the Rest of Your Life.*

Robin Ryan has been quoted or featured in most major magazines and newspapers, including *BusinessWeek, Money, Newsweek, Fortune, Good Housekeeping, USA Today,* the *Wall Street Journal,* the *New York Times,* the *Seattle Times,* the *Los Angeles Times,* and the *Chicago Tribune.*

A career counselor for more than twenty years, Robin Ryan uses her expertise daily, as she helps clients across North America land great jobs, get promotions, change careers, and secure higher salaries. A licensed vocational counselor, through telephone and in-person consultations she offers job search programs, resume writing services, salary negotiations, and interview coaching.

A highly sought-after speaker, she frequently appears at colleges, alumni gatherings, corporate training sessions, and association conferences.

Robin Ryan holds a master's degree in counseling and education from Suffolk University and a bachelor's degree in sociology from Boston College. She is the former director of counseling services at the University of Washington.

Contact Robin Ryan at 425.226.0414 or visit her website at www.robinryan.com.